Van Zanten

D0218204

Active Writing

Timothy   H.   Robinson
St. Edward's University

Laurie Modrey
Austin Community College

MACMILLAN PUBLISHING COMPANY
New York

Copyright © 1986, Macmillan Publishing Company, a division of Macmillan, Inc.

Printed in the United States of America

All rights reserved. No part of this book may be reproduced or transmitted in any form or by any means, electronic or mechanical, including photocopying, recording, or any information storage and retrieval system, without permission in writing from the Publisher.

Macmillan Publishing Company
866 Third Avenue, New York, New York 10022

Collier Macmillan Canada, Inc.

Library of Congress Cataloging in Publication Data

Robinson, Timothy H.
   Active writing.

    1. English language—Rhetoric. 2. English language—
Text-books for foreign speakers. I. Modrey, Laurie.
II. Title.
PE1408.R637 1986   808'.042   85-11473
ISBN 0-02-402510-0

Printing: 3 4 5 6 7 8   Year: 8 9 0 1 2 3 4 5

Acknowledgments

ARTHUR C. CLARKE, "The Electronic Revolution." Reprinted by permission of the author and the author's agents, Scott Meredith Literary Agency, Inc., 845 Third Avenue, New York, New York 10022.

HERBERT E. DOIG, "The Hunting Ethic" from *The Conservationist,* November 1971. Reprinted with permission.

ISBN 0-02-402510-0

JAMES F. FIXX, From *The Complete Book of Running.* Copyright © 1977 by James F. Fixx. Reprinted by permission of Random House, Inc.

JOHN HOSTETLER, "An Amish Wedding" from *Amish Society,* pp. 173–176, The Johns Hopkins University Press. Copyright © 1963. Reprinted with permission.

JAMES A. HUSTON, "The Meaningless Mean: A Proposal to Simplify Academic Averages and Grades" from *The Chronicle of Higher Education,* January 19, 1983. Copyright © 1983 by The Chronicle of Higher Education. Reprinted with permission.

CLYDE KLUCKHOHN, "The Concept of Culture" from *Mirror for Man,* pp. 17–27. Copyright © 1949 McGraw-Hill Book Company. Reproduced with permisson of the publisher.

RICHARD LARSON, "Discovery Through Questioning: A Plan for Teaching Rhetorical Invention" from *College English,* Vol. 30, No. 2 (November 1968), pp. 26–34. Reprinted by permission of author and National Council of Teachers of English.

MARY T. MADDEN, "Nursing Practices—From Dublin to London to England," pp. 778–779. Copyright © 1968, *American Journal of Nursing Company,* April, Volume 68, No. 4. Reproduced with the Company's permission.

DESMOND MORRIS, "Salutation Displays." Reprinted from *Manwatching: A Field Guide to Human Behavior,* text © 1977 by Desmond Morris. Compilation 1977 by Elsevier Publishing Projects SA, Lausanne, and Jonathan Cape Ltd., London, published by Harry N. Abrams, Inc., New York. All rights reserved.

DONALD M. MURRAY, "The Maker's Eye: Revising Your Own Manuscript" from *The Writer,* October, 1973. Copyright © 1973. Reprinted by permission of The Writer, Inc.

JOSEPH REYNOLDS, " 'I Think (and Write in a Journal), Therefore I Am.' " Copyright © 1981 by Joseph Reynolds. Reprinted by permission of the author.

JAMES C. SIMMONS, "A Matter of Interpretation," *American Way Magazine.* Copyright © April, 1983. Reprinted by permission of the author.

W. ROSS WINTEROWD, "Experimenting with a Heuristic" from *The Contemporary Writer.* Copyright © 1975 by Harcourt Brace Jovanovich, Inc. Reprinted with permission.

Preface

Active Writing is intended to help nonnative speakers of English to learn to understand and produce the kind of academic writing required at the freshman level in universities in the United States.

Active Writing is suitable for use in a writing class that meets 3 hours per week for a semester of 15 weeks. The book can also be used in a class that meets 5 hours per week for one semester or in a two-semester class with the addition of supplemental material. Depending on the students' needs, for instance, one could use as a supplement a grammar text, a reader, or a research paper text.

RATIONALE

As writing teachers, we have long been frustrated by two circumstances that affect our teaching: (1) having to use an English as a Foreign Language (EFL) writing textbook that concentrates on grammar, to the neglect of the type and level of work required by our students in freshman composition courses; and (2) having to adapt domestic writing textbooks for the use of our foreign students. Our aims in *Active Writing* are threefold: to provide for foreign students a writing textbook that teaches students to write the university-level academic English required in freshman composition courses; to present material free of U.S. cultural expectations and, therefore, compatible with the experiences of foreign students from diverse cultural backgrounds; and to in-

v

clude current thinking on the writing process that will help students to work through their writing assignments and produce the best results.

On first glance, *Active Writing* should seem similar to many of the popular domestic textbooks on the market. This is an asset because it teaches foreign students the same information and material American students are receiving in *their* classes. At the same time, however, *Active Writing* tailors and addresses this material to the foreign student. The student is not expected to have a firm understanding of U.S. culture or values; the text is thus relatively culture free. Even though the type of writing required at a U.S. institution is taught in *Active Writing*, it does not assume that the student is familiar with U.S. traditions, values, and interests. All of the material has been arranged and modified for the international student.

STRUCTURE OF THE TEXT

A linear model of the writing process, unavoidable in any textbook, cannot capture the recursive nature of the writing process or account for individual variations. For this reason, teachers should adapt the sequencing of material to suit their individual preferences and styles. A separate teacher's manual suggests various adaptations that teachers can use. Periodic review of material during the course and/or selective reference to material focusing on particular student needs may be beneficial tactics, depending on the particular instructor, class, and student.

Active Writing should be seen as a student reference rather than as a formulaic presentation of material. Teachers are encouraged to experiment; for those who feel it is to the students' advantage to closely follow a text, *Active Writing* presents a sequence that covers writing in a prewriting, writing, and rewriting progression.

To The Student welcomes the beginning writer to the world of composition. It distinguishes between the misconceptions that beginning writers often have and the realities of writing.

Chapter 1, *Invention*, discusses the need for gathering information before the student starts to write. This chapter introduces the students to many techniques to explore the world around them, to recall information, and to discover new ideas for writing. This is an important chapter, as much of the success of a writer depends upon the material collected at this stage. The information in this chapter is frequently omitted in other writing books for foreign students.

Chapter 2, *The Thesis Statement*, explains a vital component of the academic essay. The student is shown how to develop, from the materials that have been gathered through invention activities, a statement that identifies the focus of the essay.

Chapter 3, *Design*, presents the standard conventions of the English essay. It discusses the opening paragraph, the body paragraphs, the closing paragraph, and title. Each of these sections of the essay is presented through the use of an example essay, the development of which the students follow.

Chapter 4, *Revision*, explains to the students the importance of revision and offers procedures for revising. Also included is an essay in which a professional writer gives advice on revising.

Chapter 5, *Expressive Writing*, introduces the most personal aim of writing. In this chapter, the students learn to identify and express their responses to situations that affect them. Students are also introduced to the concept of *audience* in writing.

In Chapter 6, *Persuasive Writing*, the concept of audience is expanded. Students are given practice exercises that address different types of audiences and are shown different strategies of argumentation. Three models for persuasive writing are illustrated, along with a sample essay.

Chapter 7, *Referential Writing*, covers six strategies of development for referential essays: exemplification, comparison or contrast, classification, cause or effect, process, and extended definition. Each strategy is presented through a general discussion and a sample essay.

Chapter 8, *Editing*, distinguises between revising for content and editing for surface form. Grammar, punctuation, and mechanics are covered. Chapter 8 should be considered a reference section for student use throughout the semester.

Three appendices elaborate on concepts discussed in the text. *Appendix A* demonstrates transitional words and phrases (discussed in Chapter 3) as they are used in sentences. *Appendix B* takes a student essay and follows it through three stages of revision (discussed in Chapter 4); it concludes with a final draft of that essay. *Appendix C* presents professional essays that exemplify different types of writing. Included are three persuasive essays (for use with Chapter 6) and six referential essays (for use with Chapter 7). Each essay is followed by questions for discussion.

To The Student

Student writers often believe that they cannot be successful in putting their ideas on paper. Some resist writing because their classroom experiences in the past have been discouraging. Some have a distorted perception of writing; others have only a vague idea about what writing is. All of these writers are victims of common misconceptions that interfere with their writing ability. However, once you have an accurate understanding of writing and a positive attitude toward it, you should find that composing becomes easier.

POPULAR MISCONCEPTIONS

1. *"I can't write as well as a native English speaker."* Many foreign students come to the composition class with a handicap. This handicap is not in their ability, however, but in their attitude. They often think they will never be able to compete on an equal basis with their American student counterparts. They do not realize that writing is a matter of explaining and illustrating one's ideas in a clearly organized manner. Grammar, spelling, and punctuation are important, but they are not more important than content and organization. Writers have to know what they want to say and how they will say it before they deal with the surface features of writing. You should be aware that even native speakers of English can have problems with these elements. Foreign students *can* write as successfully as English-speaking students, although foreign students might have to spend a little

more time and effort in editing their work. (See Chapter 8 for a further discussion of editing.)

2. *"Good writers are born; I don't have the talent or inspiration to write."* Students tend to believe that good writers are born with natural talent or that they are driven by inspiration to put all their thoughts on paper. Some students think that whenever good writers sit down with a pen, the words flow onto the paper without any effort. In reality, however, this is extremely rare. If you read accounts by professional writers or see their work in original drafts, you will find that they agonize over blank sheets of paper and search for words and ideas as much as any student does. But what makes successful writers different from most composition students is that they have accepted the fact that good writing is work. This should not discourage you, though. Think of all the things you have learned to do that initially took work. Running a computer program is also work for a beginner, but it can be mastered with patience and concentration.

   As you become a better writer, you no doubt will find that some of this work becomes easier, but it will always require time and effort to produce a piece of writing with which you can feel satisfied.

3. *"When I write, I write only for myself—it's not important if others like it, too."* You might feel that your writing has its own unique, private style and meaning. This might be true of writing in diaries and journals, but in academic situations, it is necessary for your professor and classmates to understand your ideas. Furthermore, in your career after you graduate, your colleagues and superiors need to be able to comprehend your written work, whether it be memos, letters, or reports. Because most of your academic writing will be of a public rather than of a personal nature, it is important that others be able to follow your ideas in print. The easiest way to enable others to follow your ideas is to use the conventional pattern of written English. The authors of this book, along with your writing teacher, hope to demonstrate the best ways to get your written ideas across to *others.*

4. *"I get poor grades in composition because Professor Wordsworth doesn't agree with my ideas."* Teachers, as do all human beings, have personal preferences and convictions on a variety of topics. But when teachers grade your papers, they are concerned with *how* you have presented your ideas rather than with *what* you believe. Your development, organization, logic, and use of the English language—not your beliefs—determine your grade on a paper. Your professor may make some comments on your paper about the subject itself, but take them as helpful suggestions rather than criticism.

5. *"I don't need a writing course. My future profession doesn't require writing."* If you are looking forward to a future profession, you are going to have to finish school first. No matter what college

or university you attend, you will be required to take at least one writing course. Being able to write is a basic academic skill. Writing courses train you to communicate on an educated level with other educated people. Just as basic lab procedures are important to science classes, basic writing abilities are important across all academic fields. Knowledge is meant to be transmitted; regardless of technological advances in video and radio communications, the primary manner of transmission is through writing.

No matter what you do in life after college, you will certainly be required to know how to communicate in writing. The business, computer science, and engineering fields (as well as all other fields) demand that their professionals know how to write well. One fact that might surprise you is that professionals in all fields consistently state that the ability to write clearly is among the most valuable skills they learned in college. Moreover, they recommend that those entering their professions have a strong background in writing.

WHAT IS WRITING?

Writing is a process.   Writing is not an activity accomplished in one sitting. Just as a house is built in stages—drafting the design, putting up the framework, adding decorative features—a paper is generated through different steps. Although the process of writing is more abstract than building a house, there are essentially three stages: *prewriting, writing,* and *rewriting.* Each of these steps is equally important and necessary.

In the *prewriting* stage, you have to gather the ideas you want to write about and then find a focal point for these ideas. The prewriting stage is discussed in Chapters 1 and 2. In the *writing* stage, you gather support for your ideas and organize these materials into a certain pattern. In this stage, you actually start giving shape to your ideas on paper. The writing stage is discussed in Chapters 5, 6, and 7. In the *rewriting* stage, you examine your work to find how you can improve it. You deal not only with the content but also with the surface features of your essay. The rewriting stage is presented in Chapters 4 and 8.

Writing is not speaking.   As you are beginning a writing course, it is helpful to keep the difference between writing and speaking in mind. While talking, your audience's gestures, expressions, comments, or questions may prompt you to modify and clarify yourself. In writing, however, you do not have the benefit of your audience's responses. What you put down on paper is all that your readers have to help them understand your topic. If they cannot follow an idea, they are not able to tell you. If they cannot tell you, you are not able to change your presentation to accommodate them. This means you have to anticipate difficulties a reader might experience in grasping your meaning or logic. In short, you need to be more careful in writing than in speaking. Once your paper leaves your hand, you have no second chances.

     Writing has different levels of style.   The formal academic writing you will be doing in a composition course is different from the kind of writing you may be used to reading. Popular weekly magazines, for example, are written in a much less formal style because they are designed to appeal to a broad cross section of the public. News magazines, celebrity magazines, and other types of popular journalism do not try to prove anything; they are meant largely to entertain and to inform in a relaxed manner. The writing you will be doing in this course and throughout your academic career, however, is different in style. The papers you do for your course work need to demonstrate your ability to make an assertion and then to support that assertion with relevant material. Popular magazines tend to be conversational and casual, whereas academic or professional writing is more objective and disciplined. Keep this distinction in mind as you are writing your papers.

A SUMMARY

The ability to write well is a skill that is learned and developed; it is not a natural trait with which a few lucky people are born. Thus, it is possible for anyone to write well. With help from your teacher and this book, you can expect to become more comfortable and confident about writing in general. It is most important to remember not to get discouraged, not to give up. Writing takes perseverance. You will not need to put in as much work as the building of the pyramids of Egypt or the Great Wall of China required, but with a fraction of the effort, you will gain great satisfaction from a paper you created by your own labor.

Timothy H. Robinson
Laurie Modrey

Contents

Chapter 8.   **EDITING** _____ *99*

APPENDICES

Invention

Discovering some aspect of your topic that interests you gives you the motivation to write a well-developed paper. It is this interest, and subsequent motivation, that makes your paper worth reading; otherwise, it may seem dead or flat to both you and your readers. This chapter will provide you with not only a variety of methods to discover ideas, but also ways to explore those ideas and aid you in the writing process. This activity of discovering and exploring ideas is called *invention.* Invention does not mean making up information, but rather learning what you truly have to say about a subject, or what aspect of it you might have to research in order to discuss a topic intelligently.

BECOMING AWARE

The first step to becoming a good writer is to become aware of the world around you. You should not only be knowledgeable about current affairs (local, national, or international) but you should also be a good observer. Just as botanists must be able to distinguish flowers and trees and ornithologists must differentiate the many varieties of birds, writers must be aware of the details of the world they live in.

Think of your daily routine: you get up, wash, dress, go to school, sit in classes, study, and finally sleep. But what of the world that you pass through while performing these activities? Do you notice the new flowers, the changing of the sun's position, or your classmates' and teachers' various moods? The aware observer notes these details and, in the process, discovers new ideas to write about. Because good writers can communicate to a reader only what they see and know, they have to be able to discover new ideas in everyday occurrences to capture and hold their readers' attention.

Journal Writing

One useful way of becoming an accurate observer is to keep a *journal.* In a journal, you record your daily reflections and observations about your environment. It is important, however, to distinguish between a journal and a diary. In a diary, you write down your private thoughts and personal activities. You might include these in a journal, but the purpose is different. In a journal, you explore your feelings and thoughts. The journal becomes a tool, sometimes even a friend, with which you seriously attempt to understand the events that occur around you and your personal reactions to them. Thus you include not only your observations but also your reflections on life.

The following journal excerpts were written by a nonnative speaker of English in her freshman composition class. Notice how she explores ideas that come out of her activities; she reflects on the meaning and implications of the events and actions around her. Note the contrast between this type of journal entry and an entry that is simply a narration of an external event.

ENTRY #1

The night I arrived at Austin seemed to be the most mysterious night I have ever experienced. When the plane landed on the airport, the first thing I found is that Austin is a small city with much fewer people than Hong Kong.

The airport is silent. There isn't any person except the few staffs and the passengers of our flight. It should be the last flight of the day, I supposed. When I stepped out of the airport, I began to get in touch with this strange but lovely place.

The first thing I did was to look at the sky because there is a Chinese idiom saying that "the moon of all places other than your own country is round." However, the sky wasn't clear that night. Even the stars hid away from me. I was so lonely!

It was already eleven o'clock. As I walked along the road, I wondered if there was any people knowing my arrival at Austin besides the immigration department officers. The day I left Hong Kong was 3rd of July, everybody was greeting me with flowers, cards, and presents from their deepest of their hearts. I missed my family. I missed my friends, moreover. I missed the place where I had stayed for seventeen years—Hong Kong. The night I arrived at Austin was also third of July. Although it was summer, I shivered.

The road before me is narrow and long. It heats your feet in shiny days and freezes them in snowy days. The lamp poles stood there straightly and calmly, watching people crying and laughing, talking and thinking, standing and sitting, winning and losing. Would someone give me a hand when I get into trouble? Probably not. I had no friends here, there were even no strange faces at that night. Warm breezes became cold sharp knives stabbing my heart through my clothes. All thoughts began to mix up. The clearest thing I remembered was the story of "The Outsider" of Albert Camus.

ENTRY #2

I wear a Polo T-shirt, jeans, and Top-Siders without socks. I step on a large piece of grassland in the university. Row upon row of delicate green now breaks the monotony of the carefully prepared beds. With at least twenty letters on my left hand and piles of new letter pads on my right hand, I sit by the tree and start replying my letters.

Once, I was sitting on a piece of grasslands reading my letters, and staying by a tree. However, the place, the time, the clothes, the letters are different. It was several months ago when I was having my break under a tree in school in Hong Kong. At that time, I was wearing my uniform and reading letters from States and Australia.

. . .

After the letter of acceptance to the girls' school in Hong Kong . . . I spent the next six years behind the bamboo trees near the fence, studying "The Struggle to Become a Person" and memorizing the school poem and some Chinese poets. The teachers were friendly but old-minded; the school rules were complete but stern.

. . .

A few months ago my secondary school studies was finished. All the school rules are thrown with my "long and loose" uniform. It was the start of another way of life; I had been exposed to no other, but free and casual university life. However, Chinese traditional discipline has ingrained in my brain which would never be erased.

Needless to say, I have experienced a great change when I stepped into the university. Instead of my usual uniform, I wore T-shirt, jeans, and colorful shoes. Looking back on my secondary school life are sources of humorous and memorable now. Even if I sometimes do the same things as before—reading beneath a tree, walking in the drizzle—my feeling may be different. Still, they were a part of my growing up, they were a part of my history.

The student who wrote these excerpts tried to relate the feelings that grew out of her observations of the events happening to her. In the first excerpt, her experiences in a new town (and new country) make her wonder about the future. She also reminisces about her former life with friends and family in her native city. In the second excerpt, the student is describing some of the changes that have occurred in her life. More important than the actual changes, however, is her realization that she is changing because of these experiences. These are examples of journal writing. Always try to get behind the surface description of an event or object to discover the impact that it has on your understanding of yourself and the world.

Besides helping to explore your environment, a journal has several practical advantages that will benefit you in your academic life. The following list presents just a few of the reasons that journal writing is so valuable to writers—students as well as professionals.

1. ***Your writing improves.***   Many aspects of writing (handwriting, spelling, even grammar, especially in a foreign language) require practice for true competence. Think back to the hours you spent in elementary school practicing writing in your native language. You might remember that learning to write required some physical and mental control. Just as daily practice in elementary school helped you learn your own language, daily practice in a journal will help you with English spelling and grammar. Thus, a journal has definite advantages for writing. Could you ever speak English fluently if you did not practice? The same situation applies to writing.

2. ***You relax about writing.***   Many people write only in response to an assignment or to send a letter to a friend. Compare this to speaking. Most people speak without any effort numerous times during the day. Writing, however, takes a certain resolution: get out the pen and paper, sit down, and then . . . what to say? A journal can help you make writing as familiar and easy as speaking. If you write ten or fifteen minutes a day in a journal, you will soon become more comfortable about writing.

3. ***Your perception of the world increases.***   When you are in the habit of writing daily, eventually you will run out of the commonplace, everyday topics that you most likely started with. At this point, your progress begins: you start to search for ideas in the world around you. When this happens, you become a true journal writer. For those who will open their eyes, the world is full of details and information.

4. ***You become more creative.***   The greatest advantage of a journal is that, by faithfully keeping one, you are able to realize the creative power that exists in writing. All of us have dreams, aspirations, hopes, fears, and doubts. All of us see life as beautiful, frustrating, demanding, and fruitful. Writing helps us discover these feelings inside us; we can use these feelings to become more creative. When our ideas blossom, we have more to write about. Instead of a chore, then, writing becomes a pleasurable activity.

The following passages are by composition students whose native language is not English. In these passages, the students are writing in their journals *about* journals. These excerpts present some feelings that you, too, will discover about a journal.

EXCERPT #1

Three more pages and my journal will be over. I remember myself say, "how boring and stupid is this homework." But now I feel it is one of the most beautiful and useful things I did during the whole semester. In addition, this journal like the one I did last semester means a lot to me because they are being the only journals I have ever had. The journal is not worth[while] because of the things it says but for the things it has made me think. . . . First, I think it is a beautiful way to keep thoughts and experiences saved so they can be analyzed and criticized by myself in another moment. Second, through the journal I have been learning to express my feelings and thoughts as clearly as possible.

EXCERPT #2

It seems like everything has an end in life and this is the end of my "dear journal."

When I first started writing on it I thought that it was awful to do it and that I was just wasting my time, but now that I am not going to write more on it I feel sorry because I got used to it and it was part of myself. Every time I felt sad I came to my journal and, believe it or not, when I wrote all my problems on it I felt much better. Maybe it is not interesting, but I feel that everytime I wrote on it I learned at least one new word in English because I didn't know it so I had to look for it in the dictionary. Thank you, professor, for doing that. Although I hate it and it took me a lot of time I think it helped me a lot!

Well, it was a pleasure. . . .

Professional writers also keep journals. In the following article, you will notice that this writer's feelings about journals are very similar to the students'.

I Think (and Write in a Journal), Therefore I Am
JOSEPH REYNOLDS

For a long time I was a reporter to a journal, of no very wide circulation, whose editor has never yet seen fit to print the bulk of my contributions, and, as is too common with writers, I got only my labor for my pains. However, in this case my pains were their own reward.

Henry David Thoreau, *Walden*

"I write, therefore I am," wrote Samuel Johnson, altering Descarte's famous dictum: "I think, therefore I am."

When writing in my journal, I feel keenly alive and somehow get a glimpse of what Johnson meant.

My journal is a storehouse, a treasury for everything in my daily life: the stories I hear, the people I meet, the quotations I like, and even the subtle signs and symbols I encounter that speak to me indirectly. Unless I capture these things in writing, I lose them.

All writers are such collectors, whether they keep a journal or not; they see life clearly, a vision we only recognize when reading their books. Thoreau exemplifies the best in journal writing—his celebrated *Walden* grew out of his journal entries.

By writing in my own journal, I often make discoveries. I see connections and conclusions that otherwise would not appear obvious to me. I become a craftsman, like a potter or a carpenter who makes a vase or a wooden stoop out of parts. Writing is a source of pleasure when it involves such invention and creation.

I want to work on my writing, too, hone it into clear, readable prose, and where better to practice my writing than in my journal. Writing, I'm told, is a skill, and improves with practice. I secretly harbor this hope. So my journal becomes the arena where I do battle with the written word.

Sometimes when I have nothing to write, I sit idly and thumb back through old entries. I rediscover incidents long forgotten.

During a recent cold midwinter night, for example, I reread an entry dated a summer ago. My wife and I had just returned after a day at the beach. We were both tired and uncomfortable after the long ride home, but our spirits were lifted when we saw our cat come down the driveway to greet us, her tail held high shouting her presence. By reading this entry, I relived the incident, warming with affection for my cat and a sunny day at the beach.

I always try to write something, however, even if it is free writing, writing anything that comes to mind. Often this process is a source of a "core idea" that can later be developed into a more finely polished piece of writing. The articles I've published had their inception in my journal.

Journal writing, in addition, is a time when I need not worry about the rules of spelling and grammar; it provides a relaxed atmosphere in which my ideas and feelings can flow freely onto the page. If I discover an idea worth developing, then my rewriting is done.

My journal becomes a place where I can try different kinds of writing, as well, from prose and poetry to letters to the editor. Attempting different kinds is useful; once I find the inspiring medium, my writing improves.

When I write in my journal, I seek the solitude of my study. With pen in hand, I become omniscient; I am aware of the quiet, damp, night air, or the early-morning sounds of life. My journal is the place where I discover life.

"Usually when a man quits writing in his journal, . . . he has lost interest in life," attests E. B. White, an inveterate journal writer himself.

So for these few moments, at least, I hold myself in hand, I am.

The most difficult part of writing a journal is beginning. You may sometimes feel that you have nothing you want to say, that your thoughts are not important enough to express, or that you do not know how you want to say something. The sight of a blank page may make your mind blank, too. If this happens to you, try one or two of the following journal-writing suggestions.

1. Think of something important that has happened to you, and describe it. Then write about your reactions. Remember that *what happened* is not as significant as *how you responded* to the occurrence. Try to examine and describe your understanding of the event and your responses to it.
2. Explore your personal viewpoint on a topic that is being discussed among your friends. Try to determine your reasons for maintaining your viewpoint.
3. Explain why you think a personal acquaintance is worthy of your praise and admiration. Conversely, you may explain why someone irritates you.
4. Try to uncover the reasons for one of your habits.
5. Pretend that you are painting with words and "draw" a person, one who is unaware of your observation. Include as many details as you can: appearance, position, personality type, and mood, for example.
6. Capture a stray thought and clarify or develop it. The more unusual the thought, the better.

These are just some suggestions to get you started. After writing a journal for a while, you should be able to sit down and start writing without any hesitation. Writing daily, without fail, is the key to journal writing.

One final note: in writing your journal entries, you should be as honest about your feelings and insights as possible. The purpose of your journal is to explore and develop yourself. The more honest you are, the more you will learn about yourself and your world.

RECALLING INFORMATION

You have already learned and assimilated a great deal of knowledge of the world, beginning from the day you were born. This section presents several techniques for recalling information to use in your writing.

Group Discussion

You have often sat around a table, talking with friends about a movie you saw, or a class you had, or just things you did that day. Friends are an invaluable resource to tap for information. With five different friends, you will probably find five different viewpoints on a subject. From discussions with friends, you are likely to pick up many different ideas and pieces of information about a subject. Use this strategy when you write. The next time you are given an assignment, discuss the topic with your friends. Ask for their attitudes and ideas about the subject. You may discover a number of facts you are not aware of, or ideas that are thought provoking. From this discussion, choose a particular aspect of the topic that interests you. This should make your paper not only more interesting to write but also more interesting to read.

PRACTICE

Meet with three to five friends or classmates and discuss the following subjects. Take notes during your discussion, and after you have finished, mark in your notes two of the ideas (for each subject) that seem the most interesting to you.

1. Space exploration.
2. World hunger.
3. Intercultural awareness.
4. The transition between childhood and adulthood.
5. Physical fitness.

Brainstorming

Brainstorming is an activity practiced by high-level business people and government officials. In concept it is quite simple: you sit and write down whatever you can think of about an idea. Then, afterwards, you separate the worthwhile information from that which is not useful. Here are three methods you can use to brainstorm.

Free Association

Focus on an idea, and write down everything that comes into your mind that is associated with that idea. Do not try to evaluate whether your associations are useful or not. Do that later, after you have finished. For example, if you thought of the word *sun*, what might be some associations? Here is a possible list:

moon	burn	night
day	desert	eclipse
light	summer	sky
hot	winter	star
yellow	heat	chemicals
red	dry	explosion

Now try to sort out those words and ideas that might be most useful or intriguing to you. Perhaps the idea of seasonal or daily changes (as exemplified by *day, night, summer, winter*) captures your attention. Your selection of this aspect of the sun could lead to a paper on cycles of nature. If you focused on such words as *dry, hot*, and *burn*, you might choose to write on a topic in meteorology. Or the words *star, chemicals*, and *explosion* could lead you to research on astronomy, or perhaps on sun types in the universe, or on sun classifications.

In this activity, and in others later on, it is important not to think in a structured fashion. Instead, free your mind and let your thoughts flow onto your paper. This might seem strange and difficult at first, but it will become easier with practice. You will also find it rewarding as you discover how many thoughts and insights about an idea you actually have.

PRACTICE

Free-associate on the following subjects. You should try to find fifteen or twenty words before you stop. After you have written your list, see if you can perceive any patterns or groupings that could lead to an interesting idea for a paper.

1. Education.
2. Nature.
3. Stamps.
4. Music.
5. Magazines.

The Branching Egg

This activity is slightly more structured than free association, but the results are the same—you recover the information you already have stored in your mind. Suppose that you are told to write about celebrations; you would write the word *celebrations* on a piece of paper and draw an oval around it (thus forming the "egg"). If the word *celebrations* causes you to think of weddings, draw a branch extending from the egg, and on it write *weddings.* With the next word that comes to mind, you have to decide whether that word is related to the word in the egg or to the word on the branch. If it is related to the word on the branch, draw another line extending from that branch. Maybe the next celebration you recall is Independence Day. Because Independence Day is related to the word in the egg, you then would draw another branch from the egg. You then think of the word *parade* —you write that word on a branch that extends from *Independence Day.* Next, *parade* might make you think of *party,* which you would attach to another branch of *Independence Day,* and to *weddings,* also. You continue doing this until you run out of ideas or associations.

The branching egg has several advantages:

1. It provides a basic framework from which you can later develop an outline.
2. It stimulates new ideas, which you discover while seeing new branches grow.
3. It allows you space to insert or add new ideas that come to you.
4. It allows you, in only five or ten minutes, to generate a quantity of information.

Consider the example in Figure 1-1, which is based on the word *celebrations.*

You can see that several kinds of celebrations, both public and personal, were generated in this egg. The primary focus of this branching egg appears to be personal celebrations. In this particular case, the writer could discard the information on Independence Day and sports championships and further develop the personal celebration theme. A topic this writer might possibly develop would be transitional stages in a person's history, which celebrations tend to mark:

birthdays → older
graduation → job
wedding → family

Another interesting topic might be a discussion of the common characteristics of these celebrations: family gatherings, gifts, parties, photographs, and food.

Figure 1-1

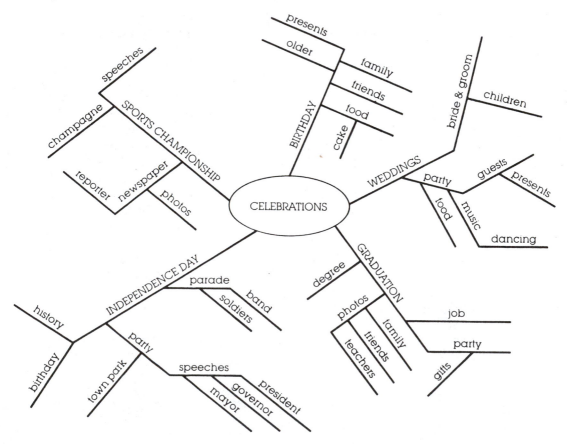

PRACTICE

Use the branching egg to recall information on the following topics. Try to develop full branches, with many extensions. If your branching egg looks more like a spider than a tree, keep on thinking. See if you can group any of your information in a way that could form the basis of an interesting paper. Some of your material should probably be discarded; you should not develop a paper that encompasses all of the information on your branches.

1. Personal budgeting.
2. Dating.
3. Careers.
4. Superstitions.
5. Television advertisements.

Free Writing

Free writing is simple. First, choose a topic—any will do. Then, sit down and start writing about that topic. From the moment you put your pen or pencil to the paper, however, do NOT stop writing. If you run out of ideas, repeat your previous sentence, or write, "I do not know what to write," or write your name. Repeat this as many times as you need to until another thought enters your mind. The secret of this activity is the nonstop writing. Let your unconscious mind take over and do your thinking. Distract the rational part of your brain with the writing itself. Often, when one thinks very hard, one has great difficulty in finding a thought. Continue writing, even nonsense, and you will be surprised at how quickly another idea, without any conscious effort on your part, is discovered. This exercise requires around fifteen minutes (depending upon your writing speed) to uncover a useful amount of material.

Free writing is very much like free association or the branching egg, except that you are writing out your thoughts in sentences. This allows you to fully develop your ideas. Because you must write continuously, however, much of your material (such as your name, or repeated sentences) will not be connected to any main idea. Just as you had to separate irrelevant from useful ideas in the previous brainstorming activities, you will have to set aside those thoughts that do not contribute to your insights or understanding of your topic.

Remember, do not stop writing. You want to bypass your consciousness and let your unconscious mind recover and develop what you have already stored.

PRACTICE

Free-write (write without stopping) for at least fifteen minutes on the following topics. Do not try to write fast, just steadily. Remember that you must keep writing, even if your ideas do not appear related or are simply meaning-less. When you are finished, pick out an idea about the topic that seems to be most dominant.

1. American food.
2. Time.
3. A roommate/friend.
4. Language learning.
5. Invention exercises.

DISCOVERING NEW IDEAS

The raw materials for writing come from observing the world and by recalling information. To creatively use these raw materials, however, you must come to a new insight or view of a topic. Gaining insight is not all that difficult, but it requires using certain invention activities you may not be accustomed to. These activities are called *heuristics*.

Heuristics are systematic procedures that help you obtain a new view of objects and ideas that you already "knew" about. Here is an example: you might have recalled all you knew about a topic, such as light bulbs, through free association, the branching egg, or free writing (note that these activities are not isolated—they can be used in conjunction with each other). Although these brainstorming activities may have resulted in your seeing ideas about light bulbs that could be fruitful, you still may not have a clear notion of where to go with the material. Heuristics, on the other hand, will help you approach a topic like light bulbs in a way that you will discover a new insight—an insight that might well develop into an interesting essay.

Heuristics are based upon asking yourself different types of questions. In answering these questions, you are led toward a greater understanding of your topic. Following are examples of different heuristic activities.

Looping

Looping begins like free writing. Sit down and write about an idea, without stopping. After fifteen minutes, stop and read what you have written. Ask yourself which sentence contains the central idea of your passage. Then underline that sentence. Start writing—again without stopping—on the idea in the underlined sentence. After fifteen more minutes, stop, reread what you have written, and underline the one sentence in your second passage that is most important. Then (you guessed it) write fifteen more minutes on that idea, without stopping. After the third loop, you end up with an idea that strikes to the core of what you want to write about. Two possible outcomes can result from a looping exercise:

1. You separate the significant from the insignificant. In other words, you pinpoint, exactly, the main idea of your topic by leaving behind the extra, unnecessary material. What you end up with might seem different from what you started with, but you can be assured that it will be direct and to the point.

2. You end up with a completely new idea. Suppose that in your first passage you wrote about a goal you scored in a soccer game. You underlined a sentence that described the cheers you heard from the crowd as you made the goal. In your second loop, you wrote how the cheers made you aware of your friends' and relatives' feelings about your accomplishment. In this passage, you underlined the sentence that told of giving your parents something to feel proud about. The third passage you wrote discussed the importance of your parents' pride. And in this passage you underlined the sentence about the value of your parents' love and support. This third idea, your gratitude toward your parents, is quite different from the original idea, that of making a goal in a soccer game. The final focus of interest, however, grew out of the first. This is perfectly all right. Remember that the point is to find the idea you want to write about. In looping, you do this by identifying the most important idea that emerges from what you have just written.

PRACTICE

Try the looping activity with the following topics. Be sure to keep writing continuously for fifteen minutes before you stop to identify the sentence containing the idea that seems most meaningful to you (remember, you need at least three passages). How does your final idea compare with the original?

1. A laboratory experiment you had problems with.
2. Religious values in your family.
3. Classical/traditional dances of your country.
4. A children's story you remember.
5. Courteous behavior in public places.

Topic Questions

Artful questioning can lead to a wealth of information. As a writer, you need to develop the skill of questioning until it becomes an automatic part of your writing process. Have you ever found, in working on a paper, that you had reached a point where you did not know what to do with the information you had gathered? If you went to your teacher with your problem, you probably found that in ten minutes or so you were able to focus on an idea. Your teacher probably asked a variety of questions that helped you clarify what you were trying to say. Thus, asking skillful questions about a topic can open an unlocked door to ideas you were previously unaware of.

The following sets of questions were developed by an English teacher to help students examine their composition topics. If you are uncertain about how to uncover ideas about a topic, first find the category into which your topic fits: either *I. Topics Without Comments*, or *II. Topics With Comments Already Attached*. Next, find the section that best suits that topic. Then, with the questions in that section, explore your topic. Remember, you are not going to write about all the information that you uncover through asking and answering these questions. The questions are to help you find the ideas that interest you most.

I. Topics that Invite Comment
 A. *Writing About Single Items (in present existence)*
  What are its precise physical characteristics (shape, dimensions, composition, etc.)?
  How does it differ from things that resemble it?
  Does it call to mind other objects we have observed earlier in our lives? Why? In what respects?
  From what points of view can it be examined?
  What sort of structure does it have?
  How do the parts of it work together?
  To what structure (class or sequence of items) does it belong?
  Who or what produced it in this form? Why?
  Who needs it?
  Who uses it? For what?
  What purposes might it serve?
  How can it be evaluated for these purposes?
 B. *Writing About Single Completed Events, or Parts of an Ongoing Process*
  Exactly what happened? (Tell the precise sequence: Who? What? When? How? Why? Who did what to whom? Why? What did what to what? How?)
  What were the circumstances in which the event occurred?
  What did they contribute to its happening?
  How was the event like or unlike similar events?
  What were its causes?
  What were its consequences?
  What does its occurrence imply? What action (if any) is called for?
  What was affected (indirectly) by it?
  What, if anything, does it reveal or emphasize about some general condition?
  To what group or class might it be assigned?
  Is it (in general) good or bad? By what standard? How do we arrive at the standard?
  How do we know about it? What is the authority for our information? How reliable is the authority? How do we know it to be reliable (or unreliable)?

How might the event have been changed or avoided?

To what other events was it connected? How?

C. *Writing About Abstract Concepts (e.g., "religion" and "socialism")*

To what specific items, groups of items, events, or groups of events does the word or phrase connect, in your experience or imagination?

What characteristics must an item or event have before the name of the concept can apply to it?

How has the term been used by writers whom you have read? How have they implicitly defined it?

Does the word have persuasive value? Does the use of it in connection with another concept seem to praise or condemn the other concept?

Are you favorably disposed to all things included in the concept? Why or why not?

D. *Writing About Collections of Items (in present existence)*

(These questions are in addition to the questions about single items, which can presumably be asked of each item in the group.)

What, exactly, do the items have in common? If they have features in common, how do they differ? How are the items related to each other, if not by common characteristics?

What is revealed about them in this way?

How may the group be divided?

What bases for division can be found?

Into what class, if any, can the group as a whole be put?

E. *Writing About Groups of Completed Events, Including Processes*

What have the events in common?

If they have features in common, how do they differ? How are the events related to each other (if they are not part of a chronological sequence)?

What is revealed by the events when taken as a group?

How can the group be divided? On what bases?

Into what class, if any, can the events taken as a group fit?

Does the group belong to any other structures than simply a larger group of similar events? (Is it part of a more inclusive chronological sequence? One more piece of evidence that may point toward a conclusion about history? And so on.)

Where can they be found?

What implications, if any, does the group of events have?

Does the group point to a need for some sort of action?

II. "Topics" with "Comments" Already Attached

A. *Writing About Propositions (statements set forth to be proved or disproved)*

What must be established for readers before they will believe it?

Into what subpropositions, if any, can it be broken down?
(What smaller assertions does it contain?)
What are the meanings of key words in it?
To what class (or classes) of propositions does it belong?
How inclusive (or how limited) is it?
What is at issue, if one tries to prove the proposition?
How can it be illustrated?
How can it be proven (by what kinds of evidence)?
What will or can be said in opposition to it?
Is it true or false? How do we know (direct observation, au-
thority, deduction, statistics, other sources)?
Why might someone disbelieve it?
What does it assume? What other propositions does it take for
granted?
What does it imply? (What follows from it?) Does it follow from
the proposition that action of some sort must be taken?
What does it reveal (signify) if true?
If it is a predictor, how probable is it? On what observations of
past experience is it based?
If it is a call to action, what are the possibilities that action
can be taken? (Is what is called for feasible?)
What are the probabilities that the action, if taken, will do
what it is supposed to do? (Will the action called for work?)

B. *Writing About Questions (interrogative sentences)*
Does the question refer to past, present, or future time?
What does the question assume (take for granted)?
From what data might answers be sought?
Why does the question arise?
What, fundamentally, is in doubt?
How can it be tested? Evaluated?
What propositions might be advanced in answer to it?
Is each proposition true?
If it is true:
What will happen in the future?
What follows from it?
Which of these predictions are possible? Probable?
What action should be taken (avoided) in consequence?
[Most of the other questions listed under "Propositions" also
apply.]

PRACTICE

Use the Topic Questions to explore the following subjects. Ask yourself as
many questions (in the appropriate category) as you need to until you have
found several new and interesting aspects of the topic. Be as persistent and
inquisitive as possible. Do not cheat yourself; you want to find ideas that you
do not already hold about the subjects.

1. A recent dream (Category I, Section A).
2. Diets (Category I, Section B).
3. Patriotism (Category I, Section C).
4. Nuclear weapons (Category I, Section D).
5. Industrial strikes (Category I, Section E).
6. People should be required to take a driving course before getting a license (Category II, Section A).
7. Why many people "follow the crowd" instead of thinking for themselves (Category II, Section B).

Varying Perspectives

The topic questions might be seen as an expanded version of questions reporters typically ask about an event: Who? What? Where? When? Why? and How? The next set of questions, in contrast, opens you up to new viewpoints on a subject—viewpoints you might not have been aware of before. In answering these questions about a given topic, you should be able to discover many new and interesting ideas about the topic.

1. *As an isolated, static entity.* Ask yourself, what features characterize it?
2. *As one among many of a class.* Ask yourself, how does it differ from others in its class?
3. *As part of a larger system.* Ask yourself, how does it fit into the larger system of which it is a part?
4. *As a process rather than a static entity.* Ask yourself, how is it changing?
5. *As a system rather than an entity.* Ask yourself, what are the parts, and how do they work together?

Here is an example of how the varying perspectives have been applied to examining a coin. Notice the many different and unusual ideas that the writer has come up with.

A COIN (U.S. PENNY)

1. *As an isolated, static entity (what features characterize it?)* About 2 mm. in diameter. 2 decimeters thick. Dark brown (copper) color. Weighs less than an ounce (determine exact weight later). Round. Smooth edges. Inscriptions on face side—"In God We Trust" and "Liberty." Image of Abraham Lincoln, 16th President of U.S. (facing to the right). Date—1982. Mint I.D.—D. Reverse side—image of Lincoln Memorial in Washington, D.C. Inscriptions—"United States of America," "E Pluribus Unum" ("One out of Many," in Latin), and "One Penny." Fairly smooth, but can feel images. Color and shininess varies. Smells like metal; metal taste, too (know from past experience).

2. *As one among many of a class (how does it differ from others in its class?)* Some U.S. coins are smaller, but others are larger. Material varies, also. Age varies, as does condition. Images and inscriptions vary on the coins, too. It has the lowest value of any of the U. S. coins. Very common, however.

3. *As part of a larger system (how does it fit into the larger system of which it is a part?)* It relates to the U. S. system of four common coins (and three less common ones). Also relates to the U. S. monetary system, which relates to the world monetary system. These coins and bills of the world provide the mechanics for the world economic system—people buy goods and services with these coins.

4. *As a process rather than a static entity (how is it changing?)* This coin is about three years old. Has grown dirtier and probably a little thinner with use. Started out as minerals in the ground. After a few more years, will probably be lost, or melted down to make new coins. I am examining it now, but will probably spend it soon and someone else will have it (someone else had it before me).

5. *As a system rather than an entity (what are the parts, and how do they work together?)* The coin is composed of many parts: the image, the inscription, the material, the size, the value, the shape. If I wanted to make a coin, I would have to consider all of these points. Using a coin is easy: you give it to someone when you buy something. Otherwise, it just sits there in my pocket or on my desk.

Possible topics from the coin exercise:

Who determines the characteristics of a coin?
How does a person get selected to be on a coin?
What is the relationship of the inscription to a particular country?
Why do the materials vary among the coins?
Why do countries have a particular number of coins?
When/why are new coin values introduced or discontinued?
Why do most countries seem to have coins?
Why are they different in their many characteristics (size, shape, color, and so on)?
How does the monetary system relate to economic conditions like inflation?
What happens with coins in international currency exchanges?
How does the exchange system work in actual operation? Is it effective? Does it have problems?
How could we track a coin's life (Title—"A Day in the Life of a U.S. Penny")?
How do minting operations work, from printing a new coin to its recall?

What type of decisions do Treasury Departments make in the production of money?

Some countries have people on coins, others have animals or plants. Why?

What can we learn about the different countries from their coins?

The value of varying perspectives is that they open up new views or angles. Not only are they useful for generating information, but the questioning itself is fun because it allows you to see things as you have never seen them before.

In this heuristic, as in the others described earlier, you gain access to a variety of ideas, all of which may be suitable to use in writing a paper. Be aware, however, that you should choose only ONE of these ideas to write about. Do NOT try to include everything you have discovered in one paper. If you do, your paper will be too broad and will lose its focus.

PRACTICE

Apply the five Varying Perspectives to the following subjects. You need not write out your information in complete sentences; just jot down the ideas. Persevere in your questioning—you want to discover new angles, new focuses. The most valuable discoveries are those that are uncommon, untraditional, even surprising.

1. A shoe.
2. Your English classroom.
3. Status symbols.
4. Cooking.
5. Telephone communications.

SUMMARY

This chapter introduced you to several techniques for discovering information and ideas for your writing assignments. With brainstorming, you are able to zero in on information that interests you about a topic. With heuristics, you will find new ways of seeing a topic. Asking yourself questions about a subject is really more important than finding answers because it urges you to explore a topic. It is important to persevere with your questions, however. Do not stop after just one or two. The more you explore, the more ideas you will discover.

Discovering ideas, however, is only the first step to writing. The following chapters will tell you how to use and shape your ideas. As you progress through each step of the writing process, you will find that good writing deserves time and attention, but it is not as difficult as you think.

The Thesis Statement

Once you have some understanding of what you want to write about, you have to start thinking about your presentation. An essential feature of this presentation is your thesis statement. Your thesis statement gives your audience a clear understanding of what your topic is and what direction the paper will take. Not only is the thesis statement a guide for your reader, but it is also a guide for you, the writer. A thesis statement provides you with a framework for the rest of the paper.

The thesis statement is made up of two parts: (1) an identification of your subject, and (2) the point you want to make about your subject. Consider the following sentence: *Strategic Arms Limitation Talks between the U.S. and the U.S.S.R. in actuality affect the welfare of all nations.* This thesis can be broken down into two parts:

Strategic Arms Limitation Talks between the U. S. and the U.S.S.R. . . .
(identification of subject)

. . . affect the welfare of all nations.
(the point you want to make about the subject)

You can also think of the thesis as containing a *TOPIC* and a *COMMENT* about that topic, as the following diagram illustrates:

Topic	Comment
Strategic Arms . . .	affect . . .

The thesis statement is important because it controls the ideas that you will present in the body of your essay. Because the thesis is so important, it must conform to certain guidelines to be effective. Good thesis statements exhibit the following characteristics:

1. ***The thesis statement makes an assertion.***   This assertion consists of two parts: the topic or subject and the comment. The comment is a viewpoint on the topic that will later be supported and substantiated in the rest of the paper. Consider this thesis: *University libraries are valuable not only for research and studying but also for socializing.* This thesis statement contains the topic, *university libraries,* and the comment, *valuable for research, studying,* and *socializing.*

2. ***The thesis statement contains a single topic–comment relationship.***   *The admissions policies of Big State University are too strict, and Big State University needs to upgrade its science facilities* should be changed to either *The admissions policies of Big State University are too strict* or *Big State University needs to upgrade its science facilities.*

3. ***The thesis statement is limited.***   The topic and its comment is narrowed so that the statement can be developed in detail within the limitations of the assignment. *Germany's destruction of the Hehe people, in the area now called Tanzania, demonstrated the ruthlessness of early German imperialism* is much better than *The colonial period in Africa demonstrated European imperialism at its worst.* The latter is far too broad a statement to cover in one essay.

4. ***The thesis statement is precise.***   The words you use should be unambiguous and clear. Abstract or vague words may cause your reader to mistake your exact meaning. *Taking the TOEFL is an awful experience* does not give your audience a clear understanding of what you want to say about your topic. *The fear, anxiety, and nervousness of taking the TOEFL may affect the test taker's performance* is more direct and precise. Words such as *terrible, wonderful, good, bad, interesting,* and *exciting* do not have exact meanings.

5. ***The thesis statement often includes guides that frame the rest of the essay.***   *Pizza Heaven is better than Pizza Palace* does not indicate what aspects of your topic you will discuss. A better thesis would be *The courteous service, the quality of food, and the colorful atmosphere of Pizza Heaven make it a better family restaurant than Pizza Palace.*

PRACTICE

1. Revise the following thesis statements by changing the abstract or vague words that are italicized into more concrete and precise words.
   a. The study of literature is *enjoyable.*
   b. Terminal illness takes a *terrible* toll on the victim's family.

    c. Balancing work and leisure activity is *good.*
    d. Many of today's fashions are quite *strange.*
    e. Intercultural *relationships* can be *rewarding.*

2. Narrow the focus of the following thesis statements.
    a. The energy situation in the world is critical.
    b. The human organism is a complex of many systems.
    c. People of all ages benefit from different recreational activities.
    d. World leaders need to confront the many current social problems.
    e. Various types of friendships fulfill several distinct psychological needs.

3. Write an appropriate comment that would make a good thesis statement for the following topics.
    a. The functions of women in a particular society (specify the society).
    b. Attitudes toward sexual behavior.
    c. Foreign student advisors.
    d. The role of technology in a profession (specify the profession).
    e. University education.

To avoid problems in framing your thesis statement, keep in mind the following cautions:

1. The thesis is not a statement of personal preference. *I like video games* does not require any support. Thus, it does not lend itself to explanation and development. Moreover, the subject is not suitable for a large audience. An alternative, *Video games are excellent tools to sharpen one's hand-eye coordination,* invites the audience to read the rest of the paper.

2. The thesis statement is not an announcement of what you will do. Expressions such as *In this paper . . . , I will discuss . . . ,* or *This essay is about . . .* are unnecessary because the purpose of a paper is to discuss or explain a topic. In addition, the use of *I* is inappropriate in most papers. Generally, writers are separate from their subjects; you should not refer to yourself in your paper.

3. The thesis is not a statement of fact or definition. These leave no room for expansion. How can you develop the statement *Leonardo da Vinci invented the flying machine?* There is nothing more to say. The thesis *Many concepts of modern flight are evident in Leonardo da Vinci's notes and sketches* gives the reader something to expect, and the writer something to develop and support.

4. The thesis statement is not a question. Assertions cannot be questions. Instead, your thesis should be an answer to a question about your topic. As a writer, it is your job to clarify your topic for your readers, not to ask them to decipher or answer questions that you pose. The question *Why are composition courses necessary?* could lead into a statement such as *Composition courses provide students with skills in transmitting information logically and coherently.*

PRACTICE

1. Determine which of the following sentences are good examples of thesis statements and which are poor. If the statement is a poor example, identify what its deficiencies are (e.g., it is a personal preference, too broad, vague, an announcement, a statement of fact, a question, or two topics).

    a. The development of Southeast Asian countries has had a varied history.

    b. Canoeing is a sport I enjoy.

    c. Starting an herb garden is easy if you follow several simple steps.

    d. This paper will focus on the effects of the 1982 Israeli invasion of Lebanon.

    e. Small colleges are preferable to large universities for students who want personal attention and contact with professors.

    f. What are the reasons a foreign student comes to the United States?

    g. Lotteries are a good source of income for a local government, and they can make the lucky winner rich.

    h. The development of the petroleum industry in Venezuela created severe problems in its agricultural production.

    i. The spring carnival festivities in many Latin American countries are exciting.

    j. Inflation is a rise in the general price level, resulting in a fall of purchasing power.

2. The following thesis statements are announcements of what the paper will do. Rewrite them. You might have to revise other elements in the sentence to make the thesis effective.

    a. The contents of this paper will present various considerations of a kidney transplantation.

    b. I am going to explain why the United States should not intervene in other nation's internal affairs.

    c. This paper is about the pros and cons of smoking.

    d. I want to discuss the role of television in child development.

    e. The rewards of a nursing career is the topic of this essay.

3. Turn the following questions into statements that have a topic and comment (and thus could be used as thesis statements).

    a. What are ways to resolve the world food crisis?

    b. Why is learning other languages important?

    c. How do parents influence their children's attitudes?

    d. Are local community leaders essential to the larger state?

    e. What kinds of services do credit cards provide their holders?

4. Write down five statements of fact (use a dictionary, almanac, and so on, if necessary). Think of a comment you could make about each topic in the factual statement. Then write a thesis statement from the topic and comment. For example: *Mexico borders the United States from the Pacific Ocean to the Gulf of Mexico. → Because of the sharing of a common border, Mexico has influenced the southwestern United States in food, language, and music.*

ASSIGNMENT

Choose specific examples of the following three subject areas. Explore them by using the Varying Perspectives, explained in Chapter 1. When you have found an idea that interests you, brainstorm to discover details and further information. Then formulate a thesis. Finally, list information that could support your thesis.

1. A person you know very well. Sometimes your feelings can interfere with your objective perception of the person. Choose someone you know well but are not emotionally attached to. Write about a classmate, for example, rather than a brother.

2. A place with which you are familiar. A place such as a city is too large to write about effectively. Restrict your choice of place to a particular part of the city, or a room in your family's home, or a favorite picnic area in a park.

3. An important event. This event can be personally or historically important; however, focus on a limited time period (such as the moment you boarded the plane), not your entire vacation. Or you could discuss your country's winning of a gold medal in a particular sport, as opposed to the Olympics in general.

Design

In Chapter 2, you learned how to formulate a thesis statement that expresses a controlling idea. In this chapter, you will learn to shape your ideas so that your reader will be able to follow your thoughts in a logical manner. Shaping your ideas means you have to organize them according to a pattern. Conventionally, an essay is built upon a three-part framework: an opening, a body, and a closing. The *opening* introduces your topic and presents your thesis statement to your reader. The *body* develops and supports your thesis with explanations and examples. Finally, the *closing* provides a smooth and coherent finish to your paper.

THE OPENING PARAGRAPH

Have you ever noticed how the first few minutes of a movie are designed to capture your attention? Movie directors can do this in several ways: panning across majestic scenery, focusing on unusual characters, or starting with fast-paced action and dramatic dialogue. These first minutes are crucial; they draw filmgoers into the picture. You, as a writer, also want to engage your audience's interest and attention. For this reason, the opening paragraph is important.

The opening paragraph has three major functions: (1) it announces your topic, (2) it captures your reader's interest, and (3) it presents your thesis. The opening paragraph is made up of two parts: an introduction and the thesis statement. Once you have developed your thesis statement (see Chapter 2), you should select an introduction to prepare your reader for the thesis. The following are examples of four standard introductions. The thesis statements are italicized.

ANECDOTE, STORY, OR PERSONAL EXPERIENCE

The memory is a little hazy today, but it's stronger than other memories of that time. It must have been about three or four in the morning. We had been watching T.V. for most of the night. All of us were tired but we couldn't go to bed until we saw it. I remember a lot of little delays and the T.V. commentator trying to keep our interest alive by talking about anything he could think of. Finally it was going to happen. The landing went O.K. and Armstrong came out. Then he stepped on the moon. Afterwards we all went out and looked up at the sky. The moon and the stars looked different than they had an hour before. *Since that morning so many years ago, my mystical fascination with space has been replaced by scientific curiosity.*

CONTRAST

"Lovers' Paradise" is its name in the travel brochures. The miles of white sand beaches lined with palm trees lure the tourist with dreams of beauty and solitude. Tropical fruit and exotic seafood promise delicious dining. Swimming, strolling, or just relaxing on this unspoiled island is the dream of the tired vacationer-to-be. From the moment the plane lands, however, the visitor is in for a rude surprise. *Rather than the beauty and serenity depicted in the brochures, the tourist is assailed by squalor and assaulted by insistent locals trying to get their share of the tourist dollar.*

NARROWING FOCUS

Since the dawn of history, the various cultures and societies of the world have followed distinct traditions. In passing down customs from one generation to the next, a people preserves its values and autonomy. Change in traditions is a natural phenomenon that occurs slowly over time as cultures come into contact with other cultures and adjust lifestyles accordingly. Recently, the world has seen a greater contact among cultures because of improved communication and transportation systems as well as growing political–economic dependence. Many cultures are finding that this greater contact is forcing a more rapid change in their traditions, in some cases causing alienation of parents and children. *An illustration of this cultural change can be seen in the family relationships of urban Mexico.*

FACTUAL SUMMARY OR DESCRIPTION

The integrated-circuit chip was first developed in 1959 by Fairchild Semiconductor. Made of silicon, only one square centimeter in size, tens of thousands of elements are contained in one of these technological wonders. Today the industry that has grown up around this modern marvel earns billions of dollars. *The integrated-*

circuit chip, the "heart and soul" of the micro-electronics industry today, has affected nearly every aspect of human life.

In most cases, any of these introductions is suitable. Keep in mind, however, that a good paper is always perceived as a coherent whole. When choosing your introduction, keep your thesis in mind. The introduction and thesis should carry the reader smoothly into the rest of your paper. If you have trouble selecting an introduction, ask your teacher for suggestions.

PRACTICE

Write introductions for the three thesis sentences you wrote for the Assignment (pages 23–24) in Chapter 2.

BODY PARAGRAPHS

Body paragraphs develop the ideas in your thesis. You might think of your thesis statement as the heart of your essay and the body paragraphs as the flesh and bone. The body paragraphs provide the details, support, and development that allow your reader to accept the assertion in your thesis statement. Each body paragraph develops a single idea that is implicitly or explicitly included in the thesis statement. This idea is announced in the *topic sentence.* The topic sentence presents the specific point that a paragraph will develop. It may appear anywhere in the paragraph, but the most effective placement for the topic sentence is usually in the first or second sentence. It is then enlarged through details and support in a unified, coherent manner.

Topic sentences grow out of the thesis statement. That is, the ideas in the topic sentences are included in the assertion of the thesis statement. Some thesis statements simply imply ideas about your subject which you could discuss in the body of your paper. For example, the thesis statement *Students often feel they lose their identities at large, state universities* suggests several possible points to explore. You could write about the use of numbers instead of names to identify students, the treatment of a student as merely one in a crowd rather than as an individual, or the effect of conformity resulting from the need to comply with rules and regulations. These are three possible examples suggested by the thesis statement, each one to be introduced in a separate topic sentence. With an implicit thesis, you always need to be careful that your topic sentences relate directly back to your thesis. You should not, for example, write about the quality of dorm food with the foregoing thesis statement.

Other thesis statements are explicit. These explicit thesis statements contain guides for structuring the body of your essay. The thesis *Zilker Park is a model city park in that it offers outdoor sports facilities, cultural programs, and opportunities to appreciate nature* clearly shows you would have at least three ideas to develop. The topic sentence of the first body paragraph would comment on the sports facilities in the park that city residents can enjoy. The topic sentence of the second body paragraph would identify cultural events presented in the park. The third topic sentence would focus on sites of natural beauty. If your thesis statement is explicit, you must make sure that in the rest of the paper you follow through with the ideas stated in that thesis. The sample thesis statement about Zilker Park commits you to write about three distinct features of the park. Do not neglect any one of them. Also, do not introduce any other feature of the park that is not identified in the thesis statement.

The following sentence outline demonstrates how topic sentences can be developed from the sample thesis statement:

OPENING PARAGRAPH

Introduction

Thesis Statement: Zilker Park is a model city park in that it offers outdoor sports facilities, cultural programs, and opportunities to appreciate nature.

BODY

Topic Sentence 1: First of all, the public can make use of the numerous athletic facilities.

Topic Sentence 2: Not only does Zilker Park offer athletic activities, but it is also the setting for varied cultural events.

Transitional Sentence: There is yet another reason why Zilker Park deserves recognition.

Topic Sentence: Several extraordinary nature spots are to be found there.

Although the thesis statement lends itself to developing three topic sentences and three body paragraphs, the body of the essay does not have to be only three paragraphs. This will be explained later in this chapter when development is discussed.

PRACTICE

1. In each of the following paragraphs, underline the sentence that functions best as the topic sentence. The first one is done for you to serve as an example.

   a. <u>Sociolinguistics is concerned with the interaction of language and setting.</u> Much work focuses on the relationship of language and social organization by examining linguistic evidence of class and status. Other work investigates individual variability among speakers as related to sociological context. Areas of investigation such as multilingualism, bilingualism, and the development of national language policies fall within the purview of sociolinguistics.

b. The structure of the violent gang can be analyzed into three different levels. At the center, on the first level, are the leaders, who—contrary to the popular idea that they could become "captains of the industry if only their energies were redirected"—are the most psychologically disturbed of all the members. These youths (who are usually between eighteen and twenty-five years old) need the gang more than anyone else, and it is they who provide it with whatever cohesive force it has. In a gang of some thirty boys there may be five or six such leaders who desperately rely on the gang to build and maintain a "rep," and they are always working to keep the gang together and in action. They enlist new members (by force), plot, and talk gang warfare most of their waking hours.

c. Very commonly, people associate superstition with the past, with very old ways of thinking that have been supplanted by modern knowledge. But new superstitions are continually coming into being and flourishing in our society. Listening to mothers in the park in the 1930's, one heard them say, "Now, don't you run out into the sun, or Polio will get you." In the 1940's, elderly people explained to one another in tones of resignation, "It was the Virus that got him down." And every year the cosmetic industry offers us new magic—cures for baldness, lotions that will give every woman radiant skin, hair coloring that will restore to the middle-aged the charm and romance of youth—results that are promised if we will just follow the simple directions. Families and individuals also have their cherished, private superstitions. You must leave by the back door when you are going on a journey, or you must wear a green dress when you are taking an examination. It is a kind of joke, of course, but it makes you feel safe.

d. My hearing doesn't go completely, but it is 90 percent ineffectual. I can usually hear the police whistle, although the crew often have to give me the signal a dozen times before I hear it and respond accordingly. Well into the swim, it is virtually impossible for me to discern words. If instruction is imperative, I try to raise the cap over my ears; the trainer has to yell at the top of his lungs, slowly and distinctly, and even then I am liable to catch only a couple of words. On the Lake Ontario swim, we hooked up giant speakers in hopes that I would be able to hear some music and ease my boredom. I never heard a note.

e. We have discussed some of the parallels between stereotypes regarding women's speech and beliefs about other groups considered "inferior" in some respect. Similarly, some observers believe that the type of speech commonly attributed to women is really characteristic of powerless groups in general, regardless of their sex. In a study of language behavior in the courtroom, William M. O'Barr and Bowman K. Atkins examined the language of witnesses of both sexes for such features as hesitation forms, use of intensifiers, and polite forms. They found that the use of the stereotypically women's language features is correlated more with social powerlessness than with sex. For both men and women, individuals with lower prestige jobs and less courtroom experience tended to use more of such features. Furthermore, experiments using transcripts of testimony with high and low frequency of these powerless features showed that witnesses using them were judged negatively—less trustworthy, less intelligent, less competent, etc. Although not directly linked to sex, powerless language was more frequent among women. The authors concluded that "women's language" and "powerless language" overlap and that "to speak like the powerless is not only typical of women because of the all-too-frequent powerless social position of many American women, but also part of the cultural meaning of speaking 'like a woman.' "

2. The topic sentences for the following paragraphs have been removed. Read the paragraphs, and for each one, write a possible topic sentence.

It is common for people to control space by marking it with their belongings

a. Books, papers, and other personal belongings are scattered around the favored site to render it more privately owned in the eyes of companions. Spreading out one's belongings is a well-known trick in public-transport situations, where a traveller tries to give the impression that seats next to him are taken. In many contexts carefully arranged personal markers can act as an effective territorial display, even in the absence of the territory owner. Experiments in a library revealed that placing a pile of magazines on the table in one seating position successfully reserved that place for an average of 77 minutes. If a sports jacket was added, draped over the chair, then the "reservation effect" lasted for over two hours.

TV can be as addictive as drugs

b. The worries and anxieties of reality are as effectively deferred by becoming absorbed in a television program as by going on a "trip" induced by drugs or alcohol. And just as alcoholics are only inchoately aware of their addiction, feeling that they control their drinking more than they really do ("I can cut it out any time I want—I just have to have three or four drinks before dinner"), people similarly overestimate their control over television watching. Even as they put off other activities to spend hour after hour watching television, they feel they could easily resume living in a different, less passive style. But somehow or other while the television set is present in their homes, the click doesn't sound. With television pleasures available, those other experiences seem less attractive, more difficult somehow.

Literature is like food – it doesn't do any good to have it ... if we don't internalize it.

c. The first is the property right you establish by paying for it, just as you pay for clothes and furniture. But this act of purchase is only the prelude to the possession. Full ownership comes only when you have made it a part of yourself, and the best way to make yourself a part of it is by writing in it. An illustration may make the point clear. You buy a beefsteak and transfer it from the butcher's icebox to your own. But you do not own the beefsteak in the most important sense until you consume it and get it into your bloodstream. I am arguing that books, too, must be absorbed in your bloodstream to do you any good.

d. As soon as mankind began to have brains they must have loved to exercise them for exercise' sake. The "jig-saw" puzzles come from China, where they had them four thousand years ago. So did the famous "sixteen puzzle" (fifteen movable squares and one empty space) over which we wracked our brains in the middle ages. The mathematical puzzles come from the Greeks who left some behind them never yet solved. For example: If Achilles is chasing a tortoise and moves at such a rate that he catches up half the distance in the first minute, and half the remaining distance in the second minute, then, as he is always moving faster than the tortoise is, he must sooner or later catch up with it. But as there is always half the distance left at the end of each minute, it is equally certain that he will never catch up with it. The Greeks died without knowing the answer.

3. Write possible topic sentences for the thesis statements you wrote for the Assignment (pages 23–24) in Chapter 2.

Unity

Each paragraph of an essay should discuss one, and only one, idea. The first topic sentence of the Zilker Park outline introduces one main idea: Zilker Park offers a variety of sports facilities. Although several specific sports facilities will be mentioned when developing this topic sentence, they are all, nonetheless, sports facilities within the park. You should not write about anything else. The topic sentence controls the details that will be discussed in the paragraph. Remember that each sentence included in the paragraph must relate to the topic sentence or another sentence within the paragraph. If a sentence does not relate, do NOT write it. Look at the following outline to see how each topic sentence controls the subpoints to be discussed in the paragraphs. Notice that each subpoint develops the point of the topic sentence.

OPENING PARAGRAPH

Introduction

Thesis Statement: Zilker Park is a model city park in that it offers outdoor sports facilities, cultural programs, and opportunities to appreciate nature.

BODY

Topic Sentence 1: First of all, the public can make use of the numerous athletic facilities.
  - natural springs swimming pool
  - soccer fields
  - hike and bike trail

Topic Sentence 2: Not only does Zilker Park offer athletic activities, but it is also the setting for varied cultural events.
  - dancing under the stars
  - theater in the park
  - musical entertainment

Transitional Sentence: There is yet another reason why Zilker Park deserves recognition.

Topic Sentence 3: Several extraordinary nature spots are to be found there.
  - Zilker Gardens
  - Barton Creek greenbelt

PRACTICE

Underline the sentences that disrupt the unity of the following paragraphs. There may be more than one inappropriate sentence to a paragraph.

1. The noise came from under a bush. As I moved a little to the left, I saw it was a big rattlesnake, the kind I saw in these parts when I was a child. When I was younger, I had also seen many deer and rabbits. He was coiled in a loose circle, his tongue darting in and out. A lot of people are afraid of snakes. The snake must have been as thick as my wrist. Because it was coiled up, I couldn't tell how big the snake was, but I wouldn't have been surprised if it was five or six feet. After a little bit I slowly stepped back, thankful that I hadn't kept on moving when I heard the rattle.

2. Smoking can be costly in more ways than the price of the package. The smoker has to buy three or four ashtrays to have around the house in various places. Then there's the cost of matches, which used to be free but not anymore, or a lighter. Disposable or refillable, the lighters are also a constant hidden drain on the bank account. Smoking also endangers the smoker's health. Perhaps most expensive is the replacing of clothes left unusable by the stray cinders dropped by the cigarette. One small hole on a shirt front makes an instant candidate for the trash out of a $30 purchase. If the same happens with furniture, a not infrequent occurrence, one is talking about hundreds of dollars.

3. Another advantage of a word-processing system over an ordinary typewriter is the mental attitude of the writer when revising. Although computers are expensive, most people can still afford them if they shop carefully. Many writers shy away from revision, necessary in any writing task, because of the work involved in retyping the project. Deleting or adding even one sentence can force a wholesale retyping of the complete text. If not, the final look is always less than satisfactory. Professors usually like their students to submit typed papers. With a word-processing system, however, the writer need have no reluctance to revise and edit the work. One can add or delete sentences, paragraphs, and even pages with a few control strokes. Even moving around sections is too easy to imagine. This simplicity in a previously time-consuming process is a benefit that one realizes in even the beginning stages of word processing.

4. After you have taken the written test, the next step is to go out "on the road." Usually the driver's license examiner will ride with you in the car. It is important that you use the seatbelt, signal all turns, and obey the speed limit. Drinking and driving is against the law in most states. Proper lane control and use of side- and rear-view mirrors are also checked. The road test will take only about 15 minutes, but it is very important in obtaining a driver's license.

5. The first measure to prevent theft loss is security. Although your doors and windows probably have locks, make sure they are strong, checked periodically, and in good working condition. Many of the locks installed in modern housing are inadequate to stop even a casual thief, to say nothing of the professional. It is not unusual for doors to be opened with plastic credit cards or a small screwdriver. Crime has risen drastically in the past few years. A deadbolt lock is the most effective way to safeguard your residence and belongings. An obvious corollary to the need for locks

is the need to use them. Even if you have the strongest lock from the hardware store or three locks on your back door, they will not protect your belongings if you do not use them. Every neighborhood has a hardware store that sells a variety of goods. Never leave your apartment unlocked, even if you expect to be away from it "only for a minute." Thieves already have many advantages—do not make them a present of your belongings.

Coherence

Paragraphs must flow together in a logical and orderly manner. You cannot merely list ideas or points at random; you must show the relationship between them. Writers use certain devices to ensure coherence, much like a mason uses mortar to cement bricks. Each idea and sentence should connect, just as bricks fit together to make a wall. The following are devices to achieve coherence.

Order
There are three ways that one can use order to aid coherence:

Time. Time order is used with events that progress through time. To give accurate directions, you have to begin with the first step and proceed chronologically. Although this may seem obvious, people often do forget important sequences in time and have to backtrack, or they may jump ahead of themselves. Examples of subjects requiring time order are historical events, political situations, or any narrative or process. Usually when using time order, you will be moving forward in time. But you may also relate events moving backward in time (reverse chronological order).

Space. Space order is used mainly in descriptions. To establish coherence, choose one direction in space and maintain it. For example, if you are describing a person, list details from head to toe or vice versa. Or, if you are describing a room, present details from left to right or right to left. There are basically three directions you can take: left to right (or the reverse); top to bottom (or the reverse); and around in a circle (clockwise). Do not skip around at random.

Importance. Order of importance is used when your ideas are not equal in weight. You can choose to present ideas in one of two ways: from most important to least important or from least important to most important. The most important points, however, are generally left to the end—to make a greater impact on the reader.

In some writing, you may not find any clear-cut order. If an order seems obvious, however, make sure you use it. When appropriate, the use of order (time order, space order, order of importance) will strengthen your writing. Assign one predominant order and maintain it throughout the paragraph or essay.

Repetitions

Repeating important words, phrases, or ideas holds your paper together by linking one thought to another. Suppose you were writing about the problems a student experiences during school registration. The repetition of words such as *irritation, frustration, difficulty,* or *anger* would provide a common thread throughout the paragraph. Not only does this help hold the paragraph together, but it stresses the feeling you want to communicate. You can not only repeat the same words or use similar words, but you can also use pronouns.

Sometimes whole sentence structures (parallelism) can be repeated for emphasis. But be careful not to overuse this device because it can become monotonous.

Transitions

Transitions are probably the most effective means of establishing coherence. Transitional words and phrases emphasize the relationship between ideas. Listed here are transitional words, which are categorized according to the types of relationships they show. (See Appendix A for sample sentences using these transitions.)

Transitional Words

Exemplification

for example	namely	that is
an example of this	specifically	a case in point
in other words	in particular	for instance
frequently	to illustrate	

Enumeration/Sequence

first, second . . .	finally	before
moreover	also	another
in addition	next	afterwards
then	after	again
furthermore	later	

Comparison

similarly	not only . . . but also
also	likewise
just as	in the same way/manner

Contrast

but	however	even though
though	nevertheless	unlike
yet	still	in contrast
on the other hand	in spite of	on the contrary
conversely	whereas	despite
in fact	although	nonetheless

Result

therefore	thus	as a consequence
consequently	as a result	for this reason

hence	for	because
accordingly	so	

Emphasis

even	actually	as a matter of fact
surely	obviously	true
certainly	again	
undoubtedly	indeed	

Summary

in summary	in conclusion	to conclude
in brief	on the whole	to summarize
to sum up	in short	

You need to use transitions in two places in your essays: within paragraphs and between paragraphs. Look at the transitions in the following paragraph:

> *Not only* does Zilker Park offer athletic activities, *but* it *also* is the setting for varied cultural events. Many of the city's dance companies, *for example,* perform on the weekends in the summer at the Hillside Theater. Austinites can see anything from "Romeo and Juliet" to experimental modern dance. Enjoying a picnic dinner while watching dance under the stars is an unforgettable experience. *In addition* to dance, it is possible to see dramatic productions at the park. Both serious and lighthearted fare are available for those who enjoy plays. *If dance or drama is not one's preference,* the wide variety of entertainment can fill an afternoon or evening. Choose from the annual musical, the jazz festival, or a classical evening; whatever choice is made, a good cross section of the Austin community will be there.

In the first sentence, the *not only . . . but also* phrase links this paragraph with the preceding paragraph on outdoor sports activities. The other three transitions in this paragraph introduce the subpoints of the theme of cultural events. They enable the sentences to flow smoothly from one thought to another and prevent abrupt changes of thought. Notice that every new subpoint is introduced by some kind of transition.

Do not rely exclusively upon one-word transitions. Make a conscious effort to use transitional phrases. You may even want to use a transitional sentence. Look at the Zilker Park outlines given on pages 28 and 31. The third topic sentence is preceded by a transitional sentence. The use of a variety of transitional devices establishes coherence and makes reading your paper easier.

PRACTICE

The two sets of sentences which follow were taken from two different paragraphs. The order of the sentences, however, has been scrambled. Read the sentences and determine their proper order. Then write the sentences in a normal paragraph form, adding the necessary transitions in the blank spaces. (First read through all of the sentences to get a feeling for what the paragraph is trying to say. Once you have determined how the sentences relate to each other, refer to the transition lists for possible words and phrases. Experiment with the transitions—try to include words and phrases you have not used before.)

1. a. _____ look up the subject heading in the latest issue and write down the promising titles and journal abbreviations.
   b. _____ get the pertinent issues from the library shelves.
   c. _____ ask the librarian where the different indexes are kept.
   d. _____ noting all the entries in one issue, go back to the older issues to find other entries until you have found what promises to be a good selection.
   e. The proper use of a periodical index is simple to learn and can aid tremendously in good research.
   f. _____ you have found the journals carried in the library, write down their call numbers.
   g. You need the correct index if you want to find the relevant articles.
   h. _____ you will need to find out which of these journals your library carries.
   i. _____ you might want to ask for a list of the different types: business, art, science, and so on.
2. a. _____ the programs are seen in their entirety, without distraction.
   b. Network television interrupts the program you are watching about every eight minutes with a variety of noisy, often ridiculous, commercials selling everything from cars to toothpaste.
   c. _____ the public stations carry no commercials at all.
   d. One of the biggest differences between public and network television involves commercials.
   e. True, there are a few minutes of announcements between programs, _____ they are informative (previews of coming shows) and not advertisements for a new frozen dinner.
   f. _____ is the action or drama of the program broken, _____the contrast between a serious drama and cats talking on the telephone is enough to send the viewer to the movie theater.

Development

As explained earlier, the purpose of the body paragraphs is to support the idea introduced in your thesis statement. Be sure to expand the topic sentences of each body paragraph with examples and details. Remember that writers are responsible for communicating their ideas as thoroughly as possible. If the reader does not understand your points, it is probably because you did not sufficiently develop your ideas. You might want to review Chapter 1 to help you generate more support for your body paragraphs.

Here is the third body paragraph of the Zilker Park essay.

There is yet another reason why Zilker Park deserves recognition. Several extraordinary nature spots are to be found there. One is Zilker Gardens, a favorite spot for those who love flowers. Here one can walk through the serenity of a Japanese-style garden, unexpected in the heart of Texas. The profusion of color in the rose garden will surely please the eye. Moreover, the yearly African violet show draws many indoor florists while the herb garden attracts those who enjoy growing their own food. A second opportunity to enjoy nature, particularly nature in its untouched state, is the Barton Creek greenbelt. Squirrels, racoons, and possums live in abundance amid the greenery of this rock-strewn riverbed. Even a short walk along the creek will refresh the urban dweller more used to condominiums and office buildings. All in all, Zilker Park is a beautiful natural retreat only a few minutes away from the center of downtown Austin.

Notice the abundance of details presented here. For instance, the first subpoint about the Zilker Park Gardens deals with a description of the style of the gardens (Japanese) and the mood it evokes (serenity). Three examples of the plants in the garden are also given (roses, African violets, herbs). Each of these plants, furthermore, is described according to what the visitor would be interested in (roses—viewing a profusion of color; African violets—growing indoor flowers; herbs—growing one's own food). The second subpoint, the Barton Creek greenbelt, also is presented in detail. *Squirrels, racoons, and possums* illustrate the kinds of animals one can find there. *Rock-strewn riverbed* attempts to recreate a picture of the area, as does *greenery.* *Refresh* describes how the *urban dweller* feels after getting away from the *condominiums and office buildings.*

Although many composition texts suggest three paragraphs for the body of an essay, the number of body paragraphs may vary. Unity requires that you devote at least one paragraph to each idea suggested in the thesis statement. If your thesis statement comments on three points, however, you do not need to limit yourself to only three paragraphs. You may find, in developing one of your body paragraphs, that you have a lot of details and support for the particular subpoints of that paragraph. In this case, you could separate your subpoints and develop each in an individual paragraph. For example, the paragraph of the Zilker Park essay beginning with *There is another reason . . .* could have been divided into two. One paragraph could have developed the Zilker Gardens in greater detail; the other could have discussed the features of the greenbelt.

Make sure you include details and illustrations when developing the subpoints of your topic sentences. The more details you have, the more developed your paper will be.

PRACTICE

1. Underline once the topic sentence, and underline twice the subpoints in each of the following paragraphs. Then circle the actual details or illustrations for each of the subpoints.

   a. Developments in the financial systems of the world illustrate another move we are making into science fiction. The "world credit unit" is an idea not that far away. One clear example is the proliferation of plastic money—credit cards. Millions of dollars exchange hands daily through the use of these money replacements made of plastic. International hotels and even small tourist spots display signs stating that they accept American Express, Mastercard, Visa, Diner's Card, and the like. One step beyond the credit card is the Electronic Funds Transfer System. Also known as EFTS, this procedure will even do away with the billing involved with the credit cards. The amount spent will be transferred automatically from a personal bank account to the store's. The user won't even need the plastic card—a thumb pressed on an electronic register will verify ownership of an account, and the different computers involved will do the rest. Eventually the use of currency and coins could be abandoned altogether.

   b. Another more appropriate name for today's newspapers could be "Adpaper." Each issue has at least one section of small-print classified ads. Included are advertisements for cars, houses, or pets. You can even advertise for a "friend" in the Personal Section. But the ads are also seen on each page in every other section. Usually they fill up to 80 percent of a "news" page (you have to look for the one or two inches of news), but sometimes these ads cover a full page. Instead of sitting down to read the latest political action of an international crisis or the fluctuation of the world currencies, you end up facing a collection of ads trying to persuade you to buy merchandise. You can find the latest in lamps, prices for an exercise club, or the newest color in couches, but where is the information on that international event you heard about? When there's more space devoted to the lunch specials on chicken and hamburgers in an advertisement for a fast-food chain than there is to the events in the world capitals, one wonders about the term "newspaper."

   c. The way my roommate eats is not his only disturbing characteristic. His style of dress is incredibly strange. Part of the problem is his care, or rather lack of care, for his clothes. He refuses to iron any of them; they all come from the laundry room in a big pile and they stay that way. His shirts are as wrinkled as a crumpled-up newspaper. His pants look like they have been slept in. To make his appearance even worse, he can't match colors. He'll wear yellow socks with green pants and a red-checked shirt. Sometimes his socks aren't even the same color—his "preferred" combination is green and blue (one on each foot!). In addition, he looks like he still needs his mother's help to get dressed. His shirts aren't always buttoned properly and usually at least half of the shirttail is hanging out. To top it all off is his hat; it looks like a discard from the garbage dump. Dirty-white in color, it's crushed on the top and has floppy edges. Whether he's going to class or to eat at a good restaurant (for him that's Burger Boy), he's always wearing his favorite head covering.

    d. Another reason foreign students study in the United States is that the degree can lead to a lucrative position with a multinational company. If the company is U.S.-based, the personnel director is assured that the student knows U.S. business practices. If the company is based outside the United States, the student is capable of understanding U.S. business practices and thus would be able to work with U.S. businessmen. Furthermore, prospective multinational employees getting a degree in the United States (not their native country) have demonstrated that they can live in a culture that is not their native environment. This proven ability to adapt to another culture is an asset highly prized by multinational companies. Whether the applicants would eventually be working in their native countries, the United States, or a third country, their studying in the United States could be a definite plus in the eyes of future employers.

2. Each of the following paragraphs lacks details; the subpoints are not sufficiently developed. Rewrite the paragraphs, adding support in the form of examples, details, and illustrations. Develop each subpoint with at least two sentences.

    a. My friend John's car is in worse condition than any I know. Almost all of the important mechanical parts need repair. (. . .) The interior looks terrible. (. . .) To look at its exterior you would think it had been in a war. (. . .) Even though the car should have been junked years ago, John still will not part with it.

    b. A second problem tourists encounter in a foreign country is with the language. At the airport, it's hard to get directions. (. . .) Also, in the hotel the visitor sometimes runs into difficulties. (. . .) A third headache is found at the shops and even the tourist sites. (. . .) Potential language difficulties should always be considered by travelers when they plan a trip.

    c. The funniest people are those who can never make a decision. At a car dealer, where perhaps it's easiest to understand their hesitations, they are spotted quickly. (. . .) But you can even see them when they are buying clothes. (. . .) Maybe the most irritating, however, are those found in the fruit section of the supermarket. (. . .) Watching indecisive shoppers can always provide a laugh.

    d. Perhaps the best pet for a young child is a kitten. First, it feels so nice. (. . .) Pleasant to touch, a kitten is also fun to play with. (. . .) The biggest advantage of a kitten is that it needs relatively little attention. (. . .) Most young children get a lot of pleasure and have few problems with a kitten.

THE CLOSING PARAGRAPH

So far, we have looked separately at the opening and the body paragraphs of the Zilker Park essay. Here, these paragraphs have been put together in essay form. Read the piece in its entirety.

The pressure of today's life is continually increasing for the average urban dweller. As cities become more and more crowded, we see an attendant increase in traffic and pollution. The pressure of city jobs also seems to grow each year. For these and other reasons, the city resident needs more than ever the refuge and release that parks can offer. As the importance of city parks is recognized, it behooves us to examine successful characteristics of popular parks. One such park—Zilker Park—is located in Austin, Texas. Zilker Park is a model city park in that it offers outdoor sports facilities, cultural programs, and opportunities to appreciate nature.

First of all, the public can make use of the numerous athletic areas. Barton Springs, the natural springs swimming pool, is the perfect refuge from the hot, Texas sun. In its cool, green water or under the shady, live oak trees growing around the pool, the park visitor can relax and enjoy both the natural and human scenery. For the more competitive person, the numerous soccer fields are filled with teams willing to let one more on the team. On Sundays, both men and women vie for the city championships. For those of a more solitary nature, the hike and bike trails along the river provide an escape from the rush of the city traffic. One can walk a dog, ride a bike, or jog at one's own pace forgetful of the chores left undone at home. Whether one wants to lose a few pounds or tone a few muscles, Zilker Park is the place to go.

Not only does Zilker Park offer athletic activities, but it is also the setting for varied cultural events. Many of the city's dance companies, for example, perform on the weekends in the summer at the Hillside Theater. Austinites can see anything from "Romeo and Juliet" to experimental modern dance. Enjoying a picnic dinner while watching dance under the stars is an unforgettable experience. In addition to dance, it is possible to see dramatic productions at the park. Both serious and lighthearted fare are available for those who enjoy plays. If dance or drama is not one's preference, the wide variety of musical entertainment can fill an empty afternoon or evening. Choose from the annual musical, the jazz festival, or a classical evening; whatever choice is made, a good cross section of the Austin community will be there.

There is yet another reason why Zilker Park deserves recognition. Several extraordinary nature spots are to be found there. One is Zilker Gardens, a favorite spot for those who love flowers. Here one can walk through the serenity of a Japanese-style garden, unexpected in the heart of Texas. The profusion of color in the rose garden will surely please the eye. Moreover, the yearly African violet show draws many indoor florists while the herb garden attracts those who enjoy growing their own food. A second opportunity to enjoy nature, particularly nature in its untouched state, is the Barton Creek greenbelt. Squirrels, racoons, and possums live in abundance amid the greenery of this rock-strewn riverbed. Even a short walk along the creek will refresh the urban dweller more used to condominiums and office buildings. All in all, Zilker Park is a beautiful natural retreat only a few minutes away from the center of downtown Austin.

How does the essay seem so far? Although the essay develops and supports its thesis statement, you are probably aware that something still seems to be missing. The third paragraph of the essay's body ends on a subpoint; the reader is left hanging. You would have the same feeling if you were disconnected during a telephone conversation. You would not know if the other person had finished talking or if the person had more to say. You do not want to make the reader of your essay feel disconnected, either. The way you solve this is with a *closing paragraph*. A closing paragraph gives the essay a feeling of completion. It sums up and ties together the ideas in your essay. This paragraph needs to be thoughtful and well-written because the closing paragraph creates the last impression your reader will have of your essay.

Your paper may end in several ways. The following are some common and effective methods:

- Restate, but in different words, your thesis and the major points in your essay.
- Discuss the significance of the assertion made in your thesis. For example, make predictions or speculations.
- Call your readers to action.

Read the following sample closing paragraph of the Zilker Park essay. Which of the above-mentioned methods did the author use to close the essay?

The combination of sports facilities, cultural offerings, and natural beauty makes Zilker Park an ideal haven for the city resident. People can recondition their bodies, broaden their minds, and reacquaint themselves with nature just a short drive from their workplaces. As cities expand and develop, and the pace of life becomes more demanding, parks will become increasingly essential to the well-being of urban people. City planners would do well to look to Zilker Park as an example of a park that serves and benefits its local residents.

Cautionary Note: Do not introduce any new thoughts in your closing paragraph. All important ideas should have been discussed in the body paragraphs. The closing paragraph should not lead the reader in a new direction; it should complete the paper.

TITLE

If you are wondering why the title is mentioned after the essay has been put together, it is because this is the best time to formulate it. It is only after you have written your essay, and know what it is about, that you can choose the most effective title. If you select a title before you start to write, you may find yourself restricted to the idea suggested in the title. So let your paper suggest a title for you, rather than imposing one on the paper.

With a few well-chosen words, your title either states directly the subject of your essay or catches the reader's attention. A title is *NOT* a sentence. Think of titles of movies—*Raiders of the Lost Ark, Star Wars, Enter the Dragon*—or even the title of this textbook. These titles capture a main theme; they do not make any statements about the subject. In most cases, the simpler the title the more effective it will be. By the way, the title chosen for the Zilker Park essay was "A Model City Park." Can you think of other titles that would have suited the essay?

PRACTICE

1. Here are some possible titles. What could be the subject matter of the essays?
   a. Applications of Biogenetics.
   b. Hamburger Crazy.
   c. Urban Development: Promise or Threat?
   d. Freshman Fears.
   e. The Plight of the International Student.
2. Using one (or several) invention strategies, generate enough ideas and information to be able to construct a thesis statement on the following topics. Write your thesis statement for each topic. Then think of an appropriate title for each.
   a. Home Computers.
   b. Human Organ Transplants.
   c. The Break-up of a Friendship.
   d. International Tourism.
   e. Apartment Living.

ASSIGNMENT

Choose one of the following five topics, and follow the rest of the directions.

1. A group event in which you participated (play, dance, sports competition, music recital, and so on).
2. A well-known figure (political, religious, or social) of this century, whose work or philosophy influenced your thoughts.
3. A place of historical importance.
4. An unresolved issue in your city.
5. The use of libraries in education.

- Examine the topic using the five varying perspectives.
- Select an idea you find the most interesting.
- Explore your discovered interest with the branching egg.
- Formulate a thesis statement.
- Choose an introduction type.
- Write the opening paragraph.
- Construct an outline for the body paragraphs. Write out each topic sentence. Have at least two subpoints for each paragraph.

Revision

So far, you have practiced invention activities and have had experience in formulating an effective thesis statement. Both of these activities are necessary before you actually write a paper. In addition, you have worked with developing the opening paragraph, the body paragraph, and the closing paragraph. This chapter will explain another important step in writing: *revision.*

Different writers may approach revision in different ways. Some revise while they are writing, going back to change words, sentences, and paragraphs while they are still working on a first draft. Another writer may write a complete draft of the paper, then stop and go back to revise the whole work.

If you are like the first writer, you have probably often been frustrated because you had difficulty completing your drafts. If you have spent time working on invention and organizational activities before you write, you should not be stopping to revise as you are writing. You should, instead, follow the practices of the second writer and put all of your ideas on paper first. This gives you a starting point, after which you can turn your first draft into a finished product. Keep in mind this practical rule: Always expect to write at least two, and sometimes three or four, drafts of a paper before you turn it in. Do not turn in your first draft of a paper. As the title of this book states, writing is an *active* process, and one vital step in this process is revision.

Revision is not just checking over your spelling and grammar. (These corrections are more properly called *editing* and will be dealt with in Chapter 8.) Revision means reading over your paper critically and objectively to discover where you need to make content changes. There are basically three activities in revision: *reorganizing, deleting,* and *adding.*

REORGANIZING

Read through your work at least once to check its organization. When you look at your paper as a whole, you may discover that your ideas are not arranged logically, or you may see a more effective method of organization. Read your paper slowly, and ask yourself the following questions. If you can answer a question with a "yes," go on to the next question. If your answer is "no," go back and make the needed changes in your paper.

- In the opening paragraph, is there an appropriate introduction (Chapter 3)?
- Is there a thesis statement that presents a topic and comment (Chapter 2)?
- Are there two or more body paragraphs that reflect a particular strategy of development (see Chapters 5–7 for further discussion on strategies of development)?
- Does each body paragraph have several subpoints that develop the topic sentence (Chapter 3)?
- Is there a closing paragraph (Chapter 3)?

Checking your organization ensures that your paper contains all the features required in a conventional essay. Even if you have included all the elements just listed, make sure they are strong enough to be perceived by another reader. Be as critical as you can about your essay. Do not hope, or assume, the audience will recognize your organization.

In long papers, and sometimes in short papers, you often need to rearrange words, sentences, paragraphs, or entire sections for a clearer organization. Because rearranging depends on the nature and the content of the paper itself, let another reader—your teacher, or a friend—see your first draft before you rewrite it. General guidelines for rearranging are difficult to offer, but if you follow these suggestions, you should not encounter serious problems.

DELETING

After you have checked your organization and have made any needed changes, your next activity is to delete irrelevant or unnecessary material. Sometimes, when you get excited by your topic, you may include more details than you need or than are required by your thesis statement or topic sentences. You may find yourself writing about something that need not be covered in your paper. This is called a *digression*, and it is a common problem for all writers. If you *do* digress, delete this material so you do not confuse or distract your reader. Ask yourself the following questions to determine if you have included any extraneous material. If you answer "no" to any of the questions, you will have to make some deletions in your paper.

- Do the ideas in the topic sentences come directly from the assertion of the thesis statement?
- Do the subpoints of the body paragraphs come directly from the main idea of each topic sentence?
- Do the examples, details, and illustrations in the body paragraphs come directly from each subpoint of the paragraph?

Deleting nonessential material in your paper ensures that it is unified. If necessary, refer to the discussion of unity in Chapter 3.

Another way to check for irrelevancies and digressions is to make an outline. You might have made an outline of your material to help organize the ideas before writing your paper. But while you were writing, some unnecessary ideas may have crept in. An outline for revision helps you recognize areas of your paper that need to be deleted. Look at Body Paragraph I of the following essay outline:

Thesis Statement: The ability to write well is essential to many aspects of our daily life.

BODY PARAGRAPHS

I. Professional Life
    A. Scientists
        1. reports (lab/research projects)
        2. professional articles
        3. research grants and proposals
    B. Teachers
        1. class handouts
        2. journal articles
    C. Business persons
        1. in-house memos
        2. customer letters
        3. financial reports
II. Personal Life
III. Academic Life

You can see here that Body Paragraphs I, II, and III refer to different areas of life in which writing is important. Subpoints A, B, and C of Body Paragraph I identify different professionals for whom effective writing is necessary. Examples 1, 2, and 3 are specific illustrations of the writing used by these professionals.

If you can make an outline like this, in which every idea falls into its proper place, you have probably done well. If you have any ideas that do not fit into an outline or are only marginally related, then you should probably delete them. All writers are reluctant to cross out material they have spent time and thought in writing; however, marginal ideas impair rather than strengthen the meaning of a paper.

ADDING

After reviewing your paper, perhaps with the help of a revision outline, you may have realized that you did not explain or illustrate some of your points sufficiently. This happens frequently, because even though you might have all the information in your mind or in your notes, you may have neglected to put all of it on paper. Before you hand in your paper, check to see if you have given your readers enough information to help them follow and understand your thoughts. Ask yourself the following questions as you reread your paper. You should answer "yes" to all of them.

- Are there enough body paragraphs to support the assertion of the thesis statement and to adequately deal with the chosen strategy of development?
- Are there enough subpoints (two or more) in each body paragraph to develop the topic sentence?
- Are there details, illustrations, and examples for each body paragraph subpoint?
- Are there transitions to connect the paragraphs and the subpoints within the paragraphs?

If you cannot answer "yes" to all of these questions, your paper needs development. You can go back to Chapter 3 for explanations on how to correct this. Doing more invention exercises, as discussed in Chapter 1, will also help you generate additional ideas and information to improve the development. Use whichever invention exercise you think most suitable for the point you want to examine. Even if your paper is well organized and contains no unnecessary material, your ideas need substantial support. This adding activity, then, is probably the most important type of revision you can make.

ADDITIONAL REVISION TIPS

When you revise is as important as *how* you revise. It is *NOT* a good idea to begin a revision immediately after you have written your paper. Instead, put aside your work for two or three days—or at least overnight—to distance yourself and gain some objectivity on what you have written. Time away from your paper allows you to read it impartially. Thus, you may recognize possible weaknesses in your presentation. This means, of course, that you should begin your first draft early enough to leave yourself time to revise.

Another way to sharpen your critical perspective on your paper is to read it aloud to a friend or friends. Make sure your friends understand that they are to point out weak areas. You may not agree with your friends' critical judgments; however, do not be too hasty to disagree. Look over your paper to see if your friends are right. Keep in mind that ultimately your reader's perceptions, not your own, will determine the success of your paper.

Use the following revision checklist before you turn in each of your assignments.

Revision Checklist

---

1. The paper has been clearly directed toward a specific audience (see Chapters 5–7).
2. The organization has taken the following points into account:
   - Aim (see Chapters 5–7)
   - Opening Paragraph
     —Introduction (see Chapter 3)
     —Thesis Statement (see Chapter 2)
   - Body Paragraphs (see Chapter 3)
     —Topic Sentences
     —Development
   - Closing Paragraph (see Chapter 3)
3. Unnecessary material has been deleted.
4. Material has been added if necessary:
   - Transitions
   - Details/Illustrations/Examples
5. The final paper has been developed by working through earlier drafts.

The importance of revision can not be overemphasized. Even if you think your paper is so good that you do not need to give it any more thought, let it sit for a day or two. Then revise it one more time.

Here is an article on revision by a professional writer and teacher of writing. The author discusses the need for revision and emphasizes the elements to pay attention to when revising. Perhaps most important, however, is the attitude that he thinks writers should have toward their work. When you revise, learn to do so with "The Maker's Eye."

The Maker's Eye: Revising Your Own Manuscripts
DONALD M. MURRAY

When students complete a first draft, they consider the job of writing done—and their teachers too often agree. When professional writers complete a first draft, they usually feel that they are at the start of the writing process. When a draft is completed, the job of writing can begin.

That difference in attitude is the difference between amateur and profes- 2.
sional, inexperience and experience, journeyman and craftsman. Peter F.
Drucker, the prolific business writer, calls his first draft "the zero draft"—after
that he can start counting. Most writers share the feeling that the first draft, and
all of those which follow, are opportunities to discover what they have to say and
how best they can say it.

To produce a progression of drafts, each of which says more and says it 3.
more clearly, the writer has to develop a special kind of reading skill. In school
we are taught to decode what appears on the page as finished writing. Writers,
however, face a different category of possibility and responsibility when they
read their own drafts. To them the words on the page are never finished. Each
can be changed and rearranged, can set off a chain reaction of confusion or
clarified meaning. This is a different kind of reading which is possibly more
difficult and certainly more exciting.

Writers must learn to be their own best enemy. They must accept the criti- 4.
cism of others and be suspicious of it; they must accept the praise of others and
be even more suspicious of it. Writers cannot depend on others. They must de-
tach themselves from their own pages so that they can apply both their caring
and their craft to their own work.

. . .

Most readers underestimate the amount of rewriting it usually takes to 5.
produce spontaneous reading. This is a great disadvantage to the student
writer, who sees only a finished product and never watches the craftsman who
takes the necessary step back, studies the work carefully, returns to the task,
steps back, returns, steps back, again and again. Anthony Burgess, one of the
most prolific writers in the English-speaking world, admits, "I might revise a
page twenty times." Roald Dahl, the popular children's writer, states, "By the
time I'm nearing the end of a story, the first part will have been reread and al-
tered and corrected at least 150 times. . . . Good writing is essentially rewriting. I
am positive of this."

Rewriting isn't virtuous. It isn't something that ought to be done. It is sim- 6.
ply something that most writers find they have to do to discover what they have
to say and how to say it. It is a condition of the writer's life.

. . .

Most writers scan their drafts first, reading as quickly as possible to catch 7.
the larger problems of subject and form, then move in closer and closer as they
read and write, reread and rewrite.

The first thing writers look for in their drafts is *information.* They know that 8.
a good piece of writing is built from specific, accurate, and interesting information. The writer must have an abundance of information from which to construct a readable piece of writing.

Next writers look for *meaning* in the information. The specifics must build 9.
to a pattern of significance. Each piece of specific information must carry the
reader toward meaning.

Writers reading their own drafts are aware of *audience.* They put them- 10.
selves in the reader's situation and make sure that they deliver information
which a reader wants to know or needs to know in a manner which is easily

digested. Writers try to be sure that they anticipate and answer the questions a critical reader will ask when reading the piece of writing.

11.   Writers make sure that the *form* is appropriate to the subject and the audience. Form, or genre, is the vehicle which carries meaning to the reader, but form cannot be selected until the writer has adequate information to discover its significance and an audience which needs or wants that meaning.

12.   Once writers are sure the form is appropriate, they must then look at the *structure,* the order of what they have written. Good writing is built on a solid framework of logic, argument, narrative, or motivation which runs through the entire piece of writing and holds it together. This is the time when many writers find it most effective to outline as a way of visualizing the hidden spine by which the piece of writing is supported.

13.   The element on which writers may spend a majority of their time is *development.* Each section of a piece of writing must be adequately developed. It must give readers enough information so that they are satisfied. How much information is enough? That's as difficult as asking how much garlic belongs in a salad. It must be done to taste, but most beginning writers underdevelop, underestimating the reader's hunger for information.

. . .

14.   As writers read and reread, write and rewrite, they move closer and closer to the page until they are doing line-by-line editing. Writers read their own pages with infinite care. Each sentence, each line, each clause, each phrase, each word, each mark of punctuation, each section of white space between the type has to contribute to the clarification of meaning.

15.   Slowly the writer moves from word to word, looking through language to see the subject. As a word is changed, cut, or added, as a construction is rearranged, all the words used before that moment and all those that follow that moment must be considered and reconsidered.

16.   Writers often read aloud at this stage of the editing process, muttering or whispering to themselves, calling on the ear's experience with language. Does this sound right—or that? Writers edit, shifting back and forth from eye to page to ear to page. I find I must do this careful editing in short runs, no more than fifteen or twenty minutes at a stretch, or I become too kind with myself. I begin to see what I hope is on the page, not what actually is on the page.

17.   This sounds tedious if you haven't done it, but actually it is fun. Making something right is immensely satisfying, for writers begin to learn what they are writing about by writing. Language leads them to meaning, and there is the joy of discovery, of understanding, of making meaning clear as the writer employs the technical skills of language.

. . .

18.   The maker's eye moves back and forth from word to phrase to sentence to paragraph to sentence to phrase to word. The maker's eye sees the need for variety and balance, for a firmer structure, for a more appropriate form. It peers into the interior of the paragraph, looking for coherence, unity, and emphasis, which make meaning clear.

. . .

19.   The maker's eye is never satisfied, for each word has the potential to ignite new meaning. This article has been twice written all the way through the writing

process, and it was published four years ago. Now it is to be republished in a book. The editors made a few small suggestions, and then I read it with my maker's eye. Now it has been re-edited, re-revised, re-read, re-re-edited, for each piece of writing to the writer is full of potential and alternatives.

A piece of writing is never finished. It is delivered to a deadline, torn out of the typewriter on demand, sent off with a sense of accomplishment and shame and pride and frustration. If only there were a couple more days, time for just another run at it, perhaps then . . .

20.

ASSIGNMENT

1. Look at Appendix B, pages 121–126, for an example of a first draft of a paper that has been revised. The copies of the draft, entitled Reorganizing, Deleting, and Adding, show the kinds of revisions that need to be made to the paper. The last example is the finished draft.

2. Read the following essay. Use the examples in Appendix B as a guide to reorganize, delete, and add material to the essay, in order to produce a final draft. Hint: The title presents a good idea of what the essay is meant to be about. Keep it in mind in your revisions. Look for problems in the opening paragraph (introduction and thesis), topic sentences, illustrations and examples, and the closing paragraph.

Beware of Advertisements

On my arrival in America, the one thing I noticed more than anything else was the tremendous amount of advertising that went on the radio, on television, on billboards, on road signs, and in magazines.

In the last two years I have become accustomed to this fact in American life, for I believe that it is a creative and necessary part of an industrial society. I noticed that what to believe in advertising, however, is not easy. For example, if someone wants to purchase something that he saw or heard about in advertisements, he has to take a lot of care because he is not sure about what he wants to buy.

Today many people are complaining that advertising is not truthful. For example, one airline has advertised that it is the fastest to New Orleans, but investigation detected that it is the only line flying that route. Sometimes advertising can be helpful, but sometimes not. For instance, if you want to make a trip somewhere and the advertisements can give you information such as the time of departure and the arrival and the cost of the trip as well.

Some other times advertising is totally the opposite of my first example. As a way of illustration, many people got involved in advertising and lost their money buying products because the items were of poor quality. All this happened because they don't understand the techniques of advertising, and they don't know if the advertisements give the real picture of the products or not.

Advertising, on the other hand, can be painful to some kind of people. As an example, children get involved in what we call advertising. For example, all the advertising that children see can influence the way in which they view the world, and they will grow up to believe that the most important thing in life is to buy and buy. A little boy cannot understand advertisements for what they are and so believes totally in what he hears. For instance, the advertisements can lead a child to oblige his parents to buy what he saw on t.v. such as food without knowing if it is healthful for him or not. This is because it is easy to manipulate the minds of children because they don't see things logically as adults do and because young minds are not mature enough to deal with the claims made by advertisers.

In conclusion, the future of advertising most likely will involve a much greater degree of public participation, and all consumers must take real care about the quality of the things that they want to buy, as well as the quantity. And children need their parents' guidance, not the guidance of advertisers.

Expressive Writing

What will you do with the ideas and examples generated by the activities in Chapter 1? You may want to examine and discuss your own feelings about a subject (expressive writing), or you may want to persuade your readers to see an issue your way (persuasive writing), or you may want to share information you have discovered (referential writing). Before picking up your pen, you must first determine your primary reason or aim for communicating. Moreover, this decision helps you choose your organization, support, and style. You should also determine who your intended readers are before writing. In effective prose, the aim and audience complement each other. In the next three chapters, we will examine how these two vital aspects of writing—the aim and audience—are interrelated. In this chapter, we will look at how aim and audience work in *expressive* writing.

Expressive writing is a personal kind of writing. It involves looking inside yourself and sorting out your emotions and attitudes about the world around you. Although it may seem that expressive writing is simply telling others how you feel, in reality you are discovering yourself. Imagine, for example, your first trip alone to another country. You probably experienced a variety of feelings: the exhilaration of something new, the pleasure of being on your own, perhaps the fear of being without the support of your friends and family, or the worry about whether your plans would develop as you had hoped. Expressive writing enables you to examine these feelings, thus making you more comfortable with them. Expressive writing not only helps you to learn more about yourself (your goals, values, and priorities), but it also allows you to open yourself to others.

Expressive writing is distinguished from other types of writing by its inward orientation: your subject matter is your personal world. You write only about your own experiences, observations, and reactions. You may certainly write about outside events and actions, but your main focus is on your personal reactions and responses. For example, if you were writing about your first day at a new school, you would include details of your surroundings and the events you observed, but you would always want to return to how they affected you.

PRACTICE

Write down three situations or incidents that drew a response from you. Identify the responses to these incidents that you can explore through expressive writing.

Example: When I walked into the student union, I realized that everyone was a stranger to me. I realized that I am alone here and have to go through the process of making new friends.

Example: Today I met someone who shares my interest in bicycle racing. Now I have a friend who understands my enthusiasm for cycling.

Although the focus of expressive writing is on your internal responses and reactions, you should identify those events and observations of the external world that make an impact on your internal world. In all situations, you have expectations, even though you might not be aware of them. Sometimes an experience will not meet your expectations, causing disappointment. For example, in your history class you may have thought that your work should have earned an *A*, but you received a *B* as a final grade. The difference between the grade you hoped for and the grade you actually received may upset, puzzle, or anger you. There are occasions, however, when your experiences will exceed your expectations. If you thought you had not performed well in a piano recital, but afterwards people in the audience and your teacher complimented you, you would be surprised and pleased. In other words, pleasure, sadness, anger, or excitement come about when your expectations are either not met or are exceeded. There are still other instances in which your hopes and desires are met, giving you a feeling of self-satisfaction or pride. For example, if you had put your energy into running for an office in an organization and were elected, you would feel rewarded. Expressive writing can help you understand your responses in these situations and thus learn more about yourself.

Sometimes, however, you may be unable to identify your responses. You may be left confused, bewildered, or simply uncertain. For instance, you may notice that you feel different when you are with people from your own culture than when you are with a group from another culture. This difference may not be easily recognizable as joy, discomfort, or fright; it may just puzzle you. Using expressive writing to explore this response will help you to clarify the feeling and discover the reasons for it.

PRACTICE

1. Identify a situation that did not meet your expectations. Specify what your expectations were, what the actual results were, and what you felt, e.g., anger, disappointment, embarrassment, or another similar feeling.
2. Think of another situation in which your expectations were exceeded. What were your expectations, what were the actual results, and what did you feel, e.g., happiness, pride, relief, or a similar feeling?
3. Think of a situation in which you received recognition. What were your thoughts before the event? Explain your feelings of self-satisfaction and pride as a result of this event. Why was this important to you? How did it affect you?
4. Identify a situation that caused you to feel uncertain, confused, or puzzled. Describe the actual feeling you had. Try to discover why you felt this way.

Because expressive writing is used primarily to stimulate your self-awareness, your audience is often limited to yourself. However, sometimes it is appropriate to share your expressive writing with others. No matter what your cultural, racial, or religious background, there are a number of human experiences common to everyone. Love, parenthood, rejection, or death are some examples. When you reveal your private responses to these instances, you share insights that may open others to their own feelings. Thus, your audience may often be expanded to include people who have had, or will have, a similar experience.

Whenever you find you have a topic appropriate to share with others, you have to rework your treatment of the topic to make it as meaningful to others as it is to yourself. In other words, you have to move away from a completely personal perception of the experience and stress the universality of it. You should relate your particular experience to the larger world by using the word *we,* or selecting more third-person words, such as *one* or *person,* which will identify you as part of a group. In addition, you need to be particularly careful to choose exact descriptions and to include more extensive explanations, especially as your readers might not have yet experienced a similar situation. Present your responses as part of universal human experience rather than as strictly personal experience.

PRACTICE

1. Identify which of the following passages were written for an individual audience (the writer alone) and which are directed to a larger audience. Point out the specific characteristics that indicate the passages are for one or the other audience.
   a. When I was seventeen my sister died very suddenly of an unusual illness. No one expected such a young and active girl to die. Although at

the time I thought I could never get through a day without anger, fear, disbelief, or tears, the experience forced me to reflect upon the value of human existence. It seems to me that people should remember their lost loved ones, just as I remember my sister, by the good times they shared and the respect they felt for each other. Death does not have to mean the end of a human being. Rather it preserves in our memory the qualities that made them individual and special to us when they were alive. . . .

b. My biology teacher doesn't seem to like me very much. I think he purposely chooses to use me as a bad example. Whenever I do a procedure incorrectly during our labs, he immediately points it out to the rest of the class. He makes sarcastic comments on my exams and ignores me when I raise my hand. This simply isn't fair! He never makes fun of or criticizes anyone else. I know biology isn't my favorite subject and that my grades are not always that good, but he can't expect everyone to be a scientific genius. When he treats me so unfairly, I don't even want to try to do better. He probably wouldn't even notice if I did. . . .

c. Watching children grow, develop personalities, and learn about life can be both frightening and rewarding. From my own experience and from observing friends and relatives who have children, this seems to be a fairly common discovery. Parents want to protect their children from all the pain that human beings must experience. More often than fear, however, we feel joy at seeing them learn about their surroundings and adjust to all that is new to them. There are so many things—sounds, tastes, and other sensations—that adults are accustomed to that excite and delight children. Having children can make the everyday world more alive for adults, too. . . .

d. When I got married, I thought my husband and I would stay together forever. I'm sure all people feel this way. But for many of us, differences in interests, education, and career, plus the passage of time, cause us to lose touch with each other and to drift apart. Often it is difficult not to blame the other person for the resultant misunderstanding and separation. We think, "If only one's mate had been wise enough to change, too! If only that person had not been so selfish!" Yet, other times we feel guilty and irresponsible because we find we can no longer live with our mates. The truth is that both people have brought about the separation and neither one should be blamed. . . .

e. Although my girlfriend has a very different personality from me, I find that it is this difference that fascinates me most about her. Whereas I am conservative and cautious, she is adventurous and carefree. I am continually surprised, yet delighted, by her ever present vitality: mountain climbing, cutting classes to spend an afternoon at the beach, hang-gliding, and rollerskating across campus. When I'm with her, I realize that there is much more to life than following the patterns of conventional society. It's almost as if she has opened for me a new window to the world. . . .

2. Each of the following passages has been written from one individual's personal viewpoint. Identify the main idea or topic of each passage. Then write a new paragraph on each of the topics so that it would be meaningful for a larger audience.

a. Sometimes in the evening as I walk along a city street, I look up at the lighted windows of the apartment buildings around me and wonder what is going on behind those window shades and curtains. I always imagine that other people's lives are more glamorous or even just more satisfying than mine. Here I am, walking on the concrete sidewalk all alone while they are sitting down to feasts of wine and fine food or entertaining a gathering of artists and musicians or simply sitting on comfortable couches with someone they love. The unknowable people behind those glass panes seem to be surrounded by a warmth and security missing from my own life. They are inside while I feel shut out and isolated. I think I'm a fairly content person but the darkness seems to bring with it loneliness, disconnection, and disappointment with myself. . . .

b. At 6:30 my alarm clock wakes me up and I think, "Oh, no! Not another Monday; not another week of work!" I often wonder why I have to work five days a week. There never seems to be enough time left over to do household chores, study, read the newspaper, or just relax. Working so much wears out my ability to concentrate and be creative. In fact, I'm sure I would be a more efficient worker and contribute more to my company if I were not forced to be there for so many hours each day. I think I would really get more done if I worked only four days a week, took care of my personal business—shopping, cleaning, and running errands—on another day, and then spent two full days with a free and clear mind. Just as it is necessary to make small repairs on machines to avoid a major breakdown, it is necessary for me to take a few days of the week off from work in order to keep interested in the job and to stay good at it. . . .

c. For me, nothing is more refreshing than an afternoon at the zoo. I love to watch the visitors as well as the animals. I have to chuckle whenever I watch the children imitating the chimpanzees swinging in their tires and the gorillas scratching their noses. Seeing the children clapping and barking with the seals, I inevitably join in. Looking at the exotic animals gives me just as much pleasure. I thrill at the majestic power of the pacing tiger. The grace and gentility of the towering giraffe always surprises me. And because I cannot ignore the clownish antics of the polar bears, I toss them a marshmallow or two. . . .

The inward and exploratory nature of expressive writing does not demand as rigid a pattern of development as other types of writing. Your expressive writing, however, still needs a direction and a form. You should introduce your topics with a clear thesis statement, and you should also adhere to the principles of paragraph structure—unity, coherence, and development—described in Chapter 3. If you do want to rework your expressive papers for a larger audience, following the persuasive or referential strategies of development outlined in Chapters 6 and 7 will be helpful.

ASSIGNMENTS

1. Spend some time in a place you have never been before. Write down your impressions as you experience them. Then, write an essay in which you analyze your reactions. Try to pinpoint and explain what your feelings were.

2. Recall the day you left your family to come to the United States (or any extended period away from your family). Write an essay on what you felt at the time.

3. Some people are hard to forget. Recall to mind a person who made a strong impression on you. Discuss your attitude toward, and thoughts about, this character in an expressive way.

4. Think of a significant event that happened to you in the last week or month. In an expressive essay, explore its importance to you.

5. Read through your journal, and find a topic that could be shared with a larger audience. Rework your journal entry to make it suitable for the school newspaper or magazine (or a similar publication with an audience of your peers).

Persuasive Writing

Did you ever try to talk your parents into buying you a car? Did you need to convince them to let you study or travel in another country? Did you ever try to make friends go to a movie instead of going to a party? Or go play soccer instead of watching a game on television? If you have ever tried to change someone's mind, you have used persuasion. The process of persuasive writing begins with your perception of an issue and ends with an attempt to get others to accept your point of view.

To be persuasive, you must first understand why you are disturbed about an issue or situation. Thus, you begin working on a persuasive paper the same way you would begin an expressive piece of writing—by exploring your feelings to identify their source. Persuasive writing is different from expressive writing, however, in that you must deal with an issue that affects a larger group of people than yourself. Examples of such issues or topics are scholarship requirements for your country; the TOEFL requirements of universities in the United States; or the rights of individual, cultural, or ethnic groups to have a stronger voice in politics.

PRACTICE

1. Some of the following topics are better suited for expressive writing and some for persuasive. Identify which aim would work best for each topic. Explain why the aim you chose suits the topic.
    a. My attitude toward American music.
    b. English requirements in my school.
    c. Age requirements for movies shown at theaters.

d. International aid to refugee camps.

e. My problem with my boyfriend/girlfriend.

2. Three groups are listed here. From your experience as a member of each group, think of an issue that should be developed persuasively. Remember that these topics should be important to the whole group, not just yourself.

a. Students at your college or university.

b. Future parents.

c. Citizens of your country.

AUDIENCE

Your audience for persuasive writing should not share the same beliefs you do. If they did, you would have no one to influence and would not be accomplishing your purpose. Your purpose, remember, is to get others to accept your view on an issue.

Usually several different interest groups may be concerned about a single situation. If you try to persuade all these people, however, your paper may lose its focus. Instead, preselect one group to address; the evidence you use to support your opinions depends upon your choice of audience. For example, if you think a course should be added to your school's curriculum, you could select for your audience fellow students who might not have given this possibility much thought, but who could probably benefit from the new course. To gain their attention and support, you could write a letter to the school newspaper explaining what the students would gain from the course.

An alternative group to approach is the school administration. Even though administrators might recognize the value of the proposed course, they might oppose it on the grounds of need, finances, or staffing. In a letter to the academic dean, therefore, you would not only need to present your reasons for the addition of this class, but you would also have to respond to any possible arguments against this new course being added. In persuasive writing, you have to consider opposing viewpoints as well as your own.

PRACTICE

The following exercises require you to explore different points of view. Recognizing other people's views on an issue prepares you to persuade effectively.

1. Consider a disagreement you have had with a friend. Write your own account of the incident. Then write an account of how your friend probably viewed it.

2. Think of a type of music you do not like (e.g., new wave/punk, country

and western, opera), and then write out reasons why people who do listen to this music enjoy it.

3. If a video arcade were to be installed in a neighborhood shopping center, imagine what the following groups of people would think. Write a short paragraph for each.
   a. Neighborhood children.
   b. Parents.
   c. Owner of the arcade.
   d. Owners of the neighboring businesses.
   e. Shoppers.

STRATEGIES OF DEVELOPMENT

Persuasive writing may follow several different structures. The structure you choose depends upon the issue and your audience. As seen previously, you may encounter two kinds of audiences: that which is unaware or indifferent, and that which has an actively different opinion.

Persuading an Unaware Audience

Dealing with the unaware audience is certainly easier. Presenting your information in a logical, intelligent manner may be enough to convince them. Imagine that you notice a problem with a playground in your neighborhood park. Although the park is small, a large number of young children play in it throughout the week. What arouses your concern, however, is that the park is next to a road on which there is heavy traffic during most hours of the day. You have often seen children run into the street, chasing after balls or playing games. You think it would be safer for the children if a fence, even a small one, separated the playground from the street. Probably in this instance no one would oppose your suggestion to put up a fence. To motivate your audience to act, you need only gather enough information, such as the number of cars passing along the street, the number of children using the playground, perhaps the number of accidents that already occurred there. Then simply state the situation as you perceive it, the change you would like to see, and the reasons why this action would be beneficial.

In a persuasive paper addressed to an unaware audience, you need to state your viewpoint and then give reasons that support it. Your paper might be organized according to the following model:

OPENING

Introduction: State/describe problem
Thesis: Your proposed solution/change/view

BODY

Reason A
Reason B
Reason C

.

.

.

Reason Z

CLOSING

Summary/Call to action

With this model, your opening is particularly important. The introduction has to make your audience aware that the problem exists, and your thesis must clearly state your view. In the body, you should support your thesis with strong evidence. The closing paragraph in a persuasive paper often calls your readers to action.

PRACTICE

Think of three situations about which your audience would be unaware. For each of these situations, write a thesis statement that reflects your persuasive viewpoint. Then list three to five reasons that support your viewpoint.

Persuading an Opposing Audience

If in your investigation of a situation you come to realize there might be active opposition to your ideas, you need to present your material differently than if you were dealing with an unaware audience. For instance, think of that new course you want offered at your school. Probably the course does not exist for several reasons: (1) the administration does not think it necessary, (2) its addition might reduce class loads in other courses, or (3) hiring an instructor would require additional money. In this case, merely listing the reasons the course should be offered will not be enough to be convincing. You must also examine the reasons it is not taught. This is the way that lawyers would prepare for a trial. Not only do they have to defend their clients, but they also have to prove to the judge that the opposition is in error. In writing a persuasive paper, imagine that you are a lawyer and that your readers are the judge. To win the judge to your side, you have to refute your opponent's arguments or illustrate how the strength of your reasons outweighs any possible differences of opinion. Never ignore the opposition if there is opposition.

There are two basic approaches to persuading an opposing audience. One way is to try to overcome the opposition by proving that all of their major arguments are invalid. Suppose, for example, that you are trying to persuade your audience that women should not be discriminated against in the work force because of physical differences. If your opponents claim that women are not strong enough to work in construction, you may answer that many women are already in jobs requiring strength, such as truck driving; or that in many countries women are responsible for most of the physical labor, such as farming; or that there are many women larger and more muscular than some men. In other words, you should refute your opponents' arguments point by point.

Here is a format you can use for a point-by-point refutation:

Model 1

OPENING

Introduction
    Thesis: The death penalty should be mandatory for anyone convicted of murder.

BODY

Opposing Argument A:	Death penalty is inhumane.
Refutation A:	Death penalty is justice.
Opposing Argument B:	It doesn't deter future murders.
Refutation B:	Court/justice system hasn't used it effectively yet (too many releases /reductions of sentences).

    .
    .
    .

Opposing Argument Z:	A mistake can be made and an innocent person executed.
Refutation Z:	Trial procedures assure accurate convictions.

CLOSING

Summary/Call to action

If you use Model 1, you need to have a strong refutation for each argument that you anticipate from your audience. Most likely, each body paragraph will begin with a topic sentence that states an opposing argument. Because you want to point out the flaws in the argument, you may include a statement to that effect, either in the topic sentence itself or in the second sentence. The remainder of each body paragraph should be devoted to proving why that particular argument is not strong or valid.

In the second approach to persuading an opposing audience, you not only refute each of your opponents' major points with a counterargument, but you also present any additional ideas that support your view. Your choice of approach depends upon the issue and what you discover in your investigation of the situation. The second approach, however, is usually more effective because your additional reasons help to strengthen your own viewpoint (see Model 2).

Model 2
OPENING

Introduction
    Thesis: The death penalty should be abolished.

BODY

Presentation of
Opposing Arguments: (A → Z) (justice, . . . , deters future murders).

Refutation of
Opposing Argument A: The death penalty is inhumane; it is not justice.

.

.

.

Refutation of
Opposing Argument Z: The death penalty in actuality does not lower the murder rate.

Your Additional Reason #1: Mistakes do occur under the present justice system.

Your Additional Reason #2: A jail sentence removes the convicted person from society.

Your Additional Reason #3: Convicted murderers may be rehabilitated and become productive members of society.

.

.

.

Your Additional Reason #n: Society should show compassion to its members rather than vengeance.

CLOSING
Summary/Call to action

If you use Model 2, your first body paragraph summarizes your audience's opinions on the subject. Then, in the next several body paragraphs, you counter each of those opinions—you should probably use one paragraph for each opinion. Following these, you include several body paragraphs that detail additional reasons that support your viewpoint. Model 2 is particularly useful when you feel you have more reasons supporting your view than your audience has for its view.

Even though these models may appear distinct and clear-cut, they are only models. In other words, you will find that in most persua-

sive writing the two formats are combined or overlapped. How you
shape your essay ultimately depends upon the information you discover while exploring your topic.

PRACTICE

   Use the invention procedures in Chapter 1 to help you discover your attitudes and ideas about the following topics. Write a thesis statement that
identifies your stand on the topic. Then choose an audience that would disagree with you, making sure to limit it to a specific group of people. Next, list
your oppositions' arguments and your counterarguments. Then list any additional support for your own side. Finally, write an essay outline like those on
pages 63 or 64 incorporating the foregoing information.

1. Nations should/should not have the right to intervene in the domestic affairs of neighboring countries.
2. College students should/should not be required to live in dormitories
   during their freshman year.
3. The Immigration and Naturalization Service of the United States should/
   should not permit foreign students to work off campus.
4. An issue that is currently being discussed at your school.
5. A controversial topic in one of your journal entries.

Evidence

The success of your persuasion is often determined by the strength of
your evidence. But how do you know what evidence will be the most
convincing? Personal opinion, although it may sway a friend, will not
mean anything to an audience who does not know you. You could use
several types of evidence to persuade an audience who does not know
you:

   Personal Experience
   Facts
   Statistics
   Support from Authority

Personal Experience

If you use personal experience in your persuasive writing, you should
be careful that the experience is not unique to yourself. In other words,
the incident you use to illustrate a point should be one that your readers either could have had themselves or could accept as reasonable
proof. If, for example, you are writing a paper to convince students living in the United States to buy insurance (car, home, health), even
though it appears to be an unneeded expense, you might cite, as an
illustration of the need for it, an experience you or a friend had. You
could explain how a friend decided not to buy insurance, but after a car

accident the purchase price of the car was lost, with no chance of it ever being recovered. Personal experience is powerful evidence if your readers see that the experience could happen to them.

Facts

Facts, of course, provide excellent support. Sometimes, however, it is difficult to distinguish fact from opinion. A fact is anything that is documented and verifiable; it is an idea, observation, or statement that is universally accepted. Opinions, on the other hand, are derived from more personal experience and observation. They tend to be more subjective and open to question.

If you write *The sense of family duty and responsibility in Japan is different from that in the United States,* this is a statement of fact. No one would challenge the assertion that there are differences in the family relationships of Japan and the United States. However, if you write *The different social problems in the United States and in Japan can be traced back to the different family relationships in those countries,* this is not a statement of fact. There is probably a lot of disagreement on this issue, even among social scientists. There are many explanations for the difference in social problems in the United States and Japan.

Remember that a fact is something everyone can agree on or accept as true. Everyone will have to agree with you if you say *The temperature today is 90 degrees;* a thermometer verifies this. However, if you say *The weather today is pleasant,* not everyone will be able to agree. The meaning of the statement changes, depending upon one's personal preference. Whenever you make a statement, make sure you are able to distinguish between fact and opinion.

PRACTICE

Identify which of the following sentences are statements of fact and which are statements of opinion. Keep in mind that a statement of fact is one that everyone can agree on because of strong, conclusive evidence consistently and repeatedly found to be true. A statement of opinion can be disagreed with, even though it might make sense and seem true, because there is no conclusive evidence that guarantees its validity.

1. University athletic programs develop academic achievement because they encourage competition.
2. In July, 1799, the French and the British fought over Napoleon's attempt to occupy Egypt.
3. A person can bleed to death in one minute, even if only one major blood vessel is cut.
4. People should be able to dictate their own laws because they are the ones who must obey them.
5. Cuneiform writing of ancient Egypt derives its name from the shape of its characters, which look like wedges.
6. People who behave like nonconformists are announcing to the world that they are really insecure.

7. The threat of capital punishment is one of the strongest deterrents to crime.
8. Sickle cell anemia blocks the flow of blood to the spleen, liver, and intestines, often disabling the sufferer.
9. The Russian ballet dancer, Mikhail Baryshnikov, began his career in the Kirov Ballet and is now the artistic director of the American Ballet Theatre.
10. The cost of an efficient mass transit system is minimal considering the benefits it would bring: a reduction in traffic jams, gas consumption, maintenance costs, and the need for more extensive highways.

Statistics

Statistics are numerical data collected from investigation or research. The statements *Forty-five people were killed in automobile accidents over the recent holiday* and *Seven percent of the students who took Chemistry 101 last semester failed the course* include statistics.

To ensure that your statistics are reliable, be sure that you use the most recent figures available. For example, statistics gathered fifty years ago on the average life span of people will no longer be valid today because of all the advances that have occurred in medicine over the years.

Also, be aware that some statistics may be misleading. If a survey reveals that 57 percent of the people polled disagreed with the president's economic policy, the validity of this statistic would depend upon how many people were questioned and who they were. If only ten people responded to the poll, and eight of them belonged to an opposing political party, the statistic would not be as reliable as a survey of one thousand people with a variety of political beliefs.

PRACTICE

1. If you were writing a paper arguing for more government funds to be spent on cancer research, what statistical information could you give (i.e., what numbers and percentages do you think your audience should know about)?
2. Suppose some student group (e.g., the Math Society, International Folk Dancers, or Business Students Organization) wanted to get official recognition from your university. What statistics would help their arguments to the administration?
3. What kind of statistics would help you argue for the enlargement of a city's airport?

Support from Authority

You may also quote or cite authorities as evidence to support your ideas. Authorities are people who are prominent locally or nationally, as a result of their work in a particular field. For example, a retired military general may be a reliable authority for a paper on a military issue, but his comments should not be used in a paper dealing with educational programs. Although the general may be highly respected in his own field (the military), the intelligent audience will realize that soldiers—even if they are generals—do not know any more than their fellow citizens about educational programs. If the Secretary of Education of a country was quoted, however, one would feel more comfortable in accepting his or her statements about education. In other words, use authorities in the field appropriate to your subject. Recognition or popularity does not make a person an authority on all subjects.

PRACTICE

1. Listed here are essay topics and possible sources of authoritative information. Match the source of authority that would best be used with each topic.

   a. Volcanoes.   1. The World Bank.
   b. Test anxiety.   2. Admissions Office.
   c. Freshman student   3. American Psychological
      enrollment.   Association.
   d. Aid to developing nations.   4. National Safety Council.
   e. Traffic accident deaths.   5. International Geological Society.

2. For the following five topics, identify two possible sources of authoritative information (people, journals, or organizations).

   a. Olympics.
   b. U.S. foreign policy.
   c. Popular music trends.
   d. Organ transplants.
   e. Tourism.

Logical Fallacies

Even when you are using logic to persuade, common errors in reasoning may weaken your argument. Make sure you do not use the following logical fallacies in your papers.

Sweeping Generalization: Making too general, or all-inclusive, statements, using words like *everybody, all, nothing, only, never, always.*

- Americans eat only hamburgers and pizza.
- All foreign students are on scholarships.

Hasty Generalization: Drawing conclusions from too few examples.

- Teachers are unfair to students.
- Foreign students are better than American students in math.

Ad Hominem: Attacking or insulting your opponent instead of dealing with the issues.

- Professor Wittaker should not be rehired next semester because she is a Marxist.
- Don't vote for Senator Richmond. He has homosexual friends.

Either-Or: Oversimplifying the argument by limiting it to two alternatives. Usually there are several alternatives to every issue, especially if you examine the issue closely.

- Women are suited for either housekeeping or secretarial work.
- The U.S. should force a solution of the Middle East situation or not be involved at all.

Bandwagon: Convincing your audience to follow the crowd. Just because many people believe an idea does not make it true. Remember that several hundred years ago, most people thought the world was flat.

- Vote for Hamilton. Can hundreds be wrong?
- I don't join clubs on campus because none of my friends do.

Three caveats: *Avoid emotional, cultural, and religious appeals.* A common practice among students is to rely on their personal emotions, cultural practices, or religious tenets to support their views. You should keep in mind, however, that persuasive papers are most effective when they are logical. Lawyers do not appeal to judges' emotions to win their cases. Neither do business people depend upon sentiment when transacting a deal. If you use your personal feelings or play upon the emotions of your audience, you will probably not accomplish your aim. Academic and professional readers will only be convinced through logic and substantiation.

Arguments based on the beliefs of a particular culture create the same problem. These arguments probably will not succeed because many readers will not come from the same cultural background as you do. Many readers will probably be unfamiliar with the beliefs, traditions, and values of your culture. They may even be opposed to your beliefs. For example, people from different cultures have divergent ideas about teacher formality, the role of women in society, and family relationships. To argue persuasively, you have to adapt your reader's perspective. Therefore, you must base your arguments on the *reader's* world, not your own. This strategy holds equally true for the American student writing in Russian as it does for the Chinese student writing in English.

To argue from a religious viewpoint introduces problems as well. To construct an argument based on ethical principles is preferable. Your readers may not have the same religious beliefs as you do. Moreover, in most academic and professional circles in the United States, religious viewpoints are not commonly used in persuasive arguments. In arguing against euthanasia, you would be more convincing if your supporting arguments were based on humanitarian or legalistic principles or tenets rather than on the Koran or the Bible (or any other religious text).

Points to Remember

- Make sure your thesis statement argues for one viewpoint.
- Determine the type of audience you are addressing: unaware or opposing.
- Incorporate and acknowledge your opposition's viewpoint.
- Address your refutations to each specific opposing viewpoint.
- Support your refutation and your own viewpoints with acceptable evidence: personal experience, facts, statistics, support from authority.
- Examine your arguments for logical fallacies; replace the fallacies with more substantial and logical reasoning.
- Avoid emotional, cultural, or religious appeals.

SAMPLE PERSUASION ESSAY

Sex Education for Children

Few subjects have stirred up more controversy than that of sex. Many people refuse to discuss it. Others can talk of nothing else. Yet nothing is more important to the human race—sex guarantees our very survival and continuation as a species. But how do we learn about such an important topic? Very often, children learn about sex through the whispered comments or misinformed and crude jokes of their peers. A better alternative, for children and society, is to have sex education classes in school.

Opponents of sex education classes cite many reasons for their opposition. They think that children, especially younger ones, are not emotionally or psychologically mature enough to be taught about sex. They also fear that sex education might lead to the misuse or abuse of a child's newfound knowledge. Finally, some people believe that the only proper teachers of sex are the children's parents.

In response to the argument that children are unprepared to learn about sex, one can say that children are in fact prepared by nature to learn about sex. All children are aware of their own and others' bodies. There is no "right" age to learn about their physical beings. In fact, it is only by denying children information about their bodies that they become psychologically or emotionally unable to deal with sex. If sex is presented to children naturally and without mystery, they can accept it as readily as they do the functioning of their arms or legs. By using animals such as mice or rabbits as classroom tools, a teacher can explain what happens during pregnancy and birth. Perhaps if we taught children the wonders of the human body, we would have fewer adults with sexual problems.

To believe that sex education would lead to children abusing or misusing this knowledge perverts the notion of education. Teaching children nutrition does not create bad eating habits. Teaching the evils of racism does not promote hatred among people. Indeed, it is the lack of knowledge about sex and the body's functioning that forces children into experimentation and eventual abuse of sexual activity. If we teach children the appropriate values of sex (as an expression of love and for the procreation of the human race), we might be able to forestall many of the current tragedies among young people.

The argument that parents are the only proper teachers of sex for children would be readily accepted if in fact all parents did teach their children. Parents are often too embarrassed to talk to their own children until it is too late. Other parents refuse to discuss sex because they believe it is something evil. And even parents with good intentions, parents who do talk with their children about sex, might themselves be misinformed about the body's reproductive system. It is far better to ensure that all children are informed about sex by qualified school instructors than to hope that children might learn about it from parents.

If sex education were a standard subject in schools, it would benefit our children by enabling them to adapt socially to their playmates and friends, regardless of sex. This socialization of children in regard to sex is surely as important as any of the other subjects, attitudes, and skills that we want children to learn in school. Sex education actually promotes a healthier society, both physically and emotionally. Sex education also could alleviate our population problems by providing, especially to our young, the basic facts about how our bodies work. If nothing else, children, and the adults they grow to be, would be informed and aware of how they came to exist on this earth and how they themselves can bring others into the world. Then families could plan the number of children they want to have.

Ignorance on any subject should be abhorred. Just as we want our children to learn history and mathematics, we should also want children to understand the miracles of their bodies. With sex education in schools, we can actually lessen unfortunate incidents and help children to learn the appropriate use of their reproductive organs. Sex education should not be left to darkened rooms; it should be brought into the light of our classrooms.

ASSIGNMENT

For each of the following persuasive essay topics that you choose or are assigned, follow these steps:

1. Explore the topic with one of the invention exercises described in Chap-

ter 1 (you might also want to check facts, statistics, and authorities on the topic).

2. After examining the information gathered through the invention activities, formulate a thesis statement for your viewpoint on the topic.

3. List reasons that support your thesis.

4. Identify an audience for your paper.

5. If your audience would actively oppose your thesis, list the arguments for its viewpoint. For each of these opposing arguments, write a possible refutation.

6. Write a first draft, incorporating what you have learned about the opening paragraph, the body paragraphs, the closing paragraphs, and the title.

7. Wait at least one day, then go over your first draft, revising it for organization, deletions, and additions.

8. Write the second draft of the essay. Make sure you edit the draft before you turn it in.

Topics

- High school education should/should not be compulsory for everyone.
- National governments should/should not provide free housing for all citizens who are living below the poverty level.
- All college students should/should not be required to take at least one Fine Arts course (e.g., Music, Art, Drama, Literature).
- Protection of the environment should/should not be a factor in a country's regulation of industrial activities.
- Advertisements for tobacco products should/should not be allowed on television.

Referential Writing

As we have seen, persuasion is used to actively sway people to your point of view. Referential writing, on the other hand, is used primarily to give information to other people. Every time you prepare a report on a laboratory experiment, summarize information, discuss a topic for an essay question, or write notes for an oral report, you will be using the referential aim. The main purpose of referential writing is to give information clearly, objectively, and logically.

Because you are already familiar with referential writing from newspapers, textbooks, and instructional manuals, you will probably recognize the main characteristic that distinguishes this aim from others we have discussed: objectivity. Because referential writing is concerned with the objective presentation of information, you should avoid referring to yourself and your preferences. Use specific, concrete language that does not reflect your personal biases. In referential writing you should not make judgments about your subject matter; let your readers evaluate the data and draw their own conclusions.

AUDIENCE

As in persuasive writing, you have to determine who your audience is before beginning a referential paper. You cannot completely discover the focus of your paper until you have identified your readers. Suppose that you want to write a paper about the problems foreign students have in the United States: your general focus is their problems. Of course, there is no reason to write for foreign students who are already in the U.S.—they probably already know the problems, from first-hand experience. One possible audience would be people who think they would like to study in the U.S. Another possible audience would be American students. Either of these audiences would learn something from your paper.

After you have determined who your audience is, you should define its characteristics further. In the specific case of people interested in studying in the United States, you know they probably have not lived in the U.S. Also, they would have little factual knowledge about the United States and what living in it is like (maybe much of their information has come from movies or books). Many of these people would be seventeen or eighteen years old. Others, however, may be older (graduate students or students returning to school after being out for awhile).

If, on the other hand, you were preparing a paper focusing on the economic advantages of solar energy for the home owner, your audience would be limited to actual or potential home owners. To further specify the audience, you need to consider who would be most interested in using solar energy. Most likely these people would be well educated, concerned about environmental issues, and employed in occupations that provided enough income to make installing solar energy devices feasible. With this particular topic and focus, moreover, it would be necessary to identify the geographical location of the audience. If your readers live in Indonesia, your paper would be directed more toward the uses of solar energy for cooling purposes rather than for heating; however, if your audience is in Sweden, you would need to stress solar power as a source of heat. If you chose to address readers across the entire United States, your paper would have to be expanded to discuss multiple uses of solar energy for different parts of the nation. The content of your paper, then, depends on your audience's characteristics.

Be careful not to think of your teacher as your audience. Even though no one but the teacher may read your paper, the teacher is actually an artificial audience. Moreover, an audience of one person imposes too rigid restrictions on the development of your topic. Instead, determine who your readers will be by deciding to whom the subject will be interesting. If you keep this audience in mind, it will make writing easier and give it some practical applicability.

PRACTICE

1. Go to your college or public library to find three different popular magazines. For each, analyze in detail the audiences. The articles, ads, and letters to the editor should supply you with clues.
2. For each topic and general focus listed here, create an appropriate audience.

	Topic	*General Focus*
a.	aerobic dancing	health benefits
b.	bookkeeping or accounting	job description and responsibilities
c.	volcanic eruptions	causes

3. Determine a general focus for the topics listed here, keeping in mind the designated audience.

Topic	*Audience*
a. bluejean advertisements	high school students
b. seasonal weather variations in Japan	tourists
c. automobile safety devices	car manufacturers

STRATEGIES OF DEVELOPMENT

Referential information can be presented in many ways. Even though this section will present six separate strategies for developing material referentially, they are likely to overlap. One strategy, however, usually dominates. If readers perceive an organizing principle, they can process information more easily. The following six strategies are those most common to the academic world; therefore, they are the ones most familiar to and understandable for your reader. They are (1) *exemplification*, (2) *comparison* or *contrast*, (3) *classification*, (4) *cause* or *effect*, (5) *process*, and (6) *extended definition*.

Exemplification

Suppose you were going to write a paper with one of these thesis statements: *Foreign students study in the United States for several reasons* or *The space program can improve the quality of our lives.* The first thesis statement would require listing or enumerating the reasons why students study in the United States. The second thesis also requires a number of examples, in this case to illustrate how the space program improves the quality of our lives. In either case, a good way to prove the validity of your thesis is by coming up with clear, strong examples.

Probably the most vivid examples reflect your own experiences or observations. And because they have been part of your own experience, you know they are valid. Personal examples are acceptable and often convincing, but you need to be careful when trying to prove a point based on your personal life. It is advisable not to include more than one personal example (some teachers, in fact, advise against any personal examples). If you do use a personal example, present it objectively, as one example of a common experience.

Another type of example is a reference to something that happened to someone you know. Again, you want to present this objectively. Instead of introducing the person as "my friend Ali," it is preferable to introduce the person as "one student from Pakistan." In this way you avoid referring to a personal relationship, which some readers would find objectionable in a referential paper.

A third (and less problematic) example is the hypothetical example. A hypothetical example is one that has not actually occurred but very probably could have. It might not come directly from your own experiences and observations, but you could have heard about it or have derived it simply from common sense. For instance, for the thesis *Foreign students study in the United States for several reasons*, you could cite an example of someone getting a job with a multinational corporation. You might not know anybody who has gotten a job like this after studying in the United States, but you do know it is very possible. If you use hypothetical examples, be sure that they are reasonable.

Because examples are your primary means of supporting your thesis in an exemplification paper, you have to be concerned with two issues: quantity and quality. If you rely on only one example, it must be remarkably strong. Using several examples is usually more convincing. Two to four examples are usually enough to provide substantial support. More than four could become boring and repetitive. Many textbooks suggest using three examples, but the number of your examples should depend upon their quality. Refer back to the development section of Chapter 3 if you want reminders on how to build support. If you find that you cannot develop your examples sufficiently, use the invention techniques presented in Chapter 1 to generate more information.

Points to Remember
- Choose the types of examples that are the most appropriate for your paper.
- Determine the number of examples your essay will need.
- Make sure your examples are developed.
- Keep your examples closely related to your topic sentence and thesis.
- Save your most forceful example for last, when it will make a greater impact on your reader.

SAMPLE EXEMPLIFICATION ESSAY:
A Wealth of Pleasures

Today the world seems to be extremely consumer-oriented. Advertisements urge us to buy both luxuries and necessities. The cost of food, clothing, and shelter has risen dramatically as has the cost of education. Theater tickets, records, and cars—everything takes money. This makes us wonder if there is anything worth having today that does not cost money. We can be assured that there is, however, if we look to our folk wisdom. An old proverb rightfully tells us that "The best things in life are free."

We need only go to a park and look around at the trees, streams, rocks, and flowers to realize that the beauty of the natural world is ours if we open our eyes. We do not even have to travel great distances to find elements of nature to capture our attention and imagination. Listening to cicadas at night, gazing at the constellations, floating on a raft in a nearby lake are memorable experiences that cost us nothing, yet impart a serenity and sense of wonder that few purchased items can.

Besides the beauty of nature, the intimacy of friendship is another aspect of life that cannot be bought with coins or credit cards. Without the company and support of good friends, neither a flashy sportscar nor a good meal would mean anything. Even if we could buy anything we wanted, we would not be able to enjoy them so much without being able to share them with friends. A new tennis racket, for example, would be useless unless we had a friend to play tennis with. A new article of clothing would lose its value unless a friend could compliment us on it or praise us for getting such a good buy. Friends also offer us emotional outlets besides company. We learn to see problems, frustrations, and joys in greater perspective when we can open ourselves to our friends.

A third free gift is health. Oddly, nobody seems to think very seriously about health until getting sick or injured. Then, all too late, we recognize how much it means to us. Even an activity as simple as walking down the street can be a pleasure if we appreciate how well our bodies are functioning. Although treatment, pills, and salves may require money to restore health, most of us are born with the free gift of health.

Nature, friends, and health are three vital elements of life that come without a sales ticket. We simply have to take time out from shopping to realize there are many irreplaceable things in life whose value money cannot equal. Leave your wallet at home someday and you will see indeed that "The best things in life are free."

ASSIGNMENT

For each of the following exemplification essay topics that you choose or are assigned, follow these steps:

1. Explore the topic with one of the invention exercises described in Chapter 1.
2. After examining the information gathered through the invention activities, formulate a thesis statement.
3. Identify an audience for your paper.
4. From your invention activities, select a number of examples that would be appropriate for your thesis.
5. Write a first draft, making sure that your examples are well developed. (Pay attention to all of the other elements of the essay: the opening paragraph, the body paragraphs, the closing paragraph, and the title.)
6. Wait at least one day, then go over your first draft, revising it for organization, deletions, and additions.
7. Write the second draft of the essay. Make sure you edit the draft before you turn it in.

Suggested Writing Topics

- Traditions that are important in your culture

- Educational uses of television
- Methods of protecting your savings
- Problems that international travelers encounter
- Conflicts nations face in the process of modernization

Comparison or Contrast

Perhaps you have been asked to develop an essay on big universities and small universities, nightclub dancing and aerobic exercises, or the eye and a camera. For these topics, a useful strategy of development would be either *comparison* or *contrast*. When you compare, you look at two items that are not overtly similar, and examine those features or characteristics that make them alike. This strategy is often used to explain to your reader something unfamiliar, by likening it to a more familiar item. Contrast, on the other hand, involves looking at two similar items and examining those features that are different. In either case, if you use comparison or contrast, your strategy is a point by point examination of two objects, people, places, events, or ideas.

Two formats lend themselves to developing a paper by comparison or contrast. One of them is the *block* format. The following outline explains why it is given this name:

OPENING

Introduction
    Thesis: From a student's viewpoint, attending a large, state university is quite different from going to a small, private university.

BODY

Block A: Large, state university
    1. Facilities
    2. Student–teacher ratio
    3. Atmosphere
Block B: Small, private university
    1. Facilities
    2. Student–teacher ratio
    3. Atmosphere

As you can see, the body of the paper is separated into two blocks, one for each item you are comparing or contrasting. If you are using this format, you need at least two paragraphs in the body—one for each item or block. Each of the blocks, of course, could be divided into several paragraphs, depending upon the number of details you want to cite.

In any comparison or contrast paper, transitions are important. Although *Block A* will probably be a straightforward presentation of all the features, *Block B* will have to be handled differently because you must relate each of the features to those mentioned in *Block A.* For this reason, transitions are crucial. The first sentence of *Block B* should contain a general comparison/contrast transition to relate the two items. Then, each feature will need some kind of transition to refer it back to the appropriate feature in *Block A.* Study the following example.

OPENING

Introduction

    Thesis: From a student's viewpoint, attending a large, state university is quite different from going to a small, private university.

BODY

A. Large, state university
   1. Facilities
   2. Student–teacher ratio
   3. Atmosphere
B. *Transitional Sentence:* Probably the most obvious difference between the two types of universities is in the facilities.

    Topic Sentence #1: Although the large university generally has all the needed equipment and necessary buildings, the small university is often not as fortunate.

    Topic Sentence #2: The student–teacher ratio also varies between the two types of universities.

    Topic Sentence #3: A final point of contrast between large, state schools and smaller, private ones is in the atmosphere that one finds at each type of institution.

Another way to develop a comparison or contrast paper is by using the *alternating* format, as illustrated in the following example:

OPENING

Introduction

    Thesis: Though seemingly very dissimilar, nightclub dancing is not all that different from aerobic exercising, in terms of its social variables.

BODY

    I. Setting
       A. Dancing—loud music, bright lights, many people
       B. Exercising—same music, colorful place, people
   II. Dress
       A. Dancing—fancy but comfortable clothes
       B. Exercising—comfortable clothes, yet colorful
  III. Purpose
       A. Dancing—have fun, meet people
       B. Exercising—stay in shape, but also meet people and have fun

Because you are dealing with only one specific feature of the two items at any one time (e.g., setting, dress, or purpose), you do not have to worry as much about transitions holding the body of the essay together. Nevertheless, you still need to maintain a smooth flow between each item (*dancing* and *exercising*) when discussing the individual features (such as *setting*). Look at Chapter 3 and Appendix A to review comparison and contrast transitions.

The body of the alternating format needs to be made up of at least as many paragraphs as there are features, perhaps more if each feature in each item deserves a separate paragraph. As discussed in Chapter 3, the number of paragraphs depends upon both the number of ideas you have and how much you develop each idea.

The choice of format is up to you; the alternating format, however, allows you to develop each feature in greater detail, without losing your reader in the overall framework of your paper. With either format you should establish in your thesis statement some basis of comparison or contrast between the two items you are examining. You could, for instance, compare or contrast a truck and a horse *as a means of transportation,* but it would be very difficult to compare or contrast a television set and a horse. Nothing connects them. Also, any feature you mention for *item A* should have a corresponding feature in *item B.* You should not introduce a feature about one item that does not relate to a feature in your second item. As with exemplification, the development of each feature you are comparing or contrasting is important. Be sure to discuss each of the features in some detail.

Remember, also, that your aim is referential; therefore, you are not trying to convince your reader that one item is superior to another. If you want to convince your readers that one of the items is better than the other, you should be writing a persuasive paper (see Chapter 6).

Points to Remember

- In one paper, choose either comparison *or* contrast; do not mix the two.
- In your thesis statement, indicate your basis for comparing or contrasting.

- Be careful not to be biased in your presentation of the two different items.
- Be consistent in your use of format (block or alternating).
- Make your comparison or contrast clear by using transitions effectively.
- Because this strategy involves a point by point examination of two items, all features in *item B* should correspond with all features in *item A.*

SAMPLE COMPARISON OR CONTRAST ESSAY:
Different Perspectives on Winter

A recent spell of unseasonably cold weather brings to mind the differences between winter in the northern and southern United States. Something interesting to note is the way that the inhabitants of these different regions respond to the climatic changes. Although the winters in the North are long and bitter, northerners take this all in stride. In the South, however, the slightest drop in temperature greatly affects the lives of southerners.

People in the North are prepared for subzero temperatures. Their homes are well-insulated, their heating systems efficient, and their pipes protected. They have chains for their car tires so that the winter storms do not disrupt their everyday travel to work, school, or the grocery store.

In addition to protected homes and vehicles, the wardrobes of northerners include down jackets, long underwear, and woolen mittens to shield them from the wind and snow. Although several feet of snow may fall, ice form on windshields and windowpanes, and the wind chill factor drop to minus 20 or 30 degrees, northerners really do not complain or marvel. They simply gather together their skis, iceskates, and snowshoes and go out to enjoy the cold. After all, it is going to last from November to April.

People in the South, on the other hand, are caught off guard when severe winter weather comes their way. Since their homes are constructed to make summer temperatures more comfortable, they suffer from being ill-equipped if the thermometer goes as low as the teens or even twenties. Homeowners frantically wrap their outdoor pipes and faucets to prevent them from freezing and bursting. Indoors, they not only raise the thermostats on their heaters, but they also burn wood in their fireplaces and keep portable electric heaters around the house at the same time.

Along with the cold, the accompanying snow and ice causes many problems. Whereas the northern states are subject to severe storms, even a small amount of winter precipitation in the South creates a disaster. Unlike northerners, southerners have no window scrapers, chains, or snow tires. A light coating of snow on the road results in many accidents. Since southerners are unused to driving on ice or snow, it is common practice for businesses and schools to be let off early when snow falls or ice forms.

Southerners' wardrobes are also inadequate for drops in temperature. Because most of their clothes are light in weight, they shiver through the winter. Some resort to piling layers of shirts and sweaters and consequently look like penguins waddling down the street. Others wrap themselves in blankets like the stereotypical American Indian.

Moreover, bad winter weather, instead of being accepted as a normal condition (as it is in the North), becomes an inescapable topic of conversation. At home and at work, the first words of greeting are comments about the cold. Scheduled programs on the radio and television are interrupted every few minutes, sometimes even replaced, by weather reports and updates. Fortunately for southerners, those cold days are few. Even though winter may officially last from December to March, most days are only moderately cold.

Ironically, many northerners, no longer able to stand the snow drifts and blustery winds, migrate south, where they too become accustomed to shivering when the thermometer reads 40 degrees. Similarly, however, there are southerners tired of the 100 degree summers who pack their bags, trade in their water-skis for snow-skis, and move north. The weather, then, serves one useful purpose—the variations across the nation often encourage citizens to see different parts of the country.

ASSIGNMENT

For each of the following comparison or contrast essay topics that you choose or are assigned, follow these steps:

1. Explore the topic with one of the invention exercises described in Chapter 1.
2. After examining the information gathered through the invention activities, formulate a thesis statement that states your basis of comparison.
3. Identify an audience for your paper.
4. Determine the features you want to examine for each of your items. Make sure you can discuss the same features for each item.
5. Choose either block or alternating format.
6. Write a first draft, making sure that you use transitions in the appropriate places (also pay attention to all of the other elements of the essay: the opening paragraph, the body paragraphs, the closing paragraph, and the title).
7. Wait at least one day, then go over your first draft, revising it for organization, deletions, and additions.
8. Write the second draft of the essay. Make sure you edit the draft before you turn it in.

Suggested Writing Topics

- Important beliefs of the younger and older generations
- Roles of women in two different cultures

- Living on your own and living with your family
- Two different sides of nature
- Two different time periods in your hometown (day/night; summer/ winter; past/present; morning/night)

Classification

Classification is an extension of comparison or contrast. In classification, you examine a number of similar items to determine variations among them. Classification is unlike comparison or contrast, however, in that it examines many items at once, all of which are members of one larger set.

Almost anything can be classified: teachers, books, flowers, restaurants. And most of these sets can be classified according to any number of common characteristics. A classroom of students, for example, could be classified according to age, major, nationality, or grade point. For your classification to be meaningful and clear, however, choose only *one* common characteristic or feature, such as nationality. In this instance, your *basis of classification* is nationality.

A good classification includes all the members of a particular set. Imagine, for example, that you are trying to classify dishes or types of food that you eat at an American restaurant. Different classes might include appetizers, soups, salads, main courses, and desserts. Everything that is served at the restaurant must be put into a class. Do not leave out any members of the set. Put every member of the set into a class.

Sometimes, you may come up with three or four distinct classes, but you might not have a clear class for some remaining members. The best way to handle this situation is to label this last class "Other" and include in it the members that do not fit in your other classes. The distinguishing feature of this "Other" class is that none of the members fit into the specified classes. See the following illustration.

English Course Population *(number of students/home country)*	*Classes* *(by language)*
4—Venezuela	Spanish—7 total (Venezuela and Mexico)
3—Bahrain	Arabic—5 total (Bahrain and Saudi Arabia)
1—Greece	Chinese—7 total (Hong Kong and Taiwan)
4—Hong Kong	Other—6 total (Greece, Malaysia, Japan, and Thailand)
2—Malaysia	
3—Mexico	
3—Taiwan	
2—Japan	
2—Saudi Arabia	
1—Thailand	

In this example, you can see that the course is composed of 25 students from 10 different countries. The basis of classification is language. Classifying the students by language results in three major classes (Spanish, Arabic, and Chinese) and four smaller classes (Greek, Malaysian, Japanese, and Thai). The four smaller classes were then grouped into a larger class, entitled "Other." The number of members in each of these last four smaller classes is not enough to be significant. The final classes are nicely divided into four roughly approximate units—and all the students in the course have been put into a class.

Be sure that you are able to divide the larger set into three or more smaller classes. If the set can be divided into only two classes, you should be using comparison or contrast instead. Conversely, do not create too many classes. Four or five classes are usually sufficient. More than four or five classes may obscure the similarities among the classes of the set.

Points to Remember

- Use only one basis of classification throughout your paper.
- Your classification system should include *all* members in your set; do not leave out any members.
- Divide your subject into three or more classes.
- Avoid using excessive classes.

SAMPLE CLASSIFICATION ESSAY:

A Place for Everyone

Anyone who has ever traveled or been a tourist in a new city has encountered hotels. If one is not camping out or staying with relatives, a hotel is the only place to end up at night. There is obviously a range to be found among the different hotels around the world, but one soon realizes that they generally fall into several types. Looking at hotels according to their amenities and service to their guests, we see that all hotels fit into four categories.

The most ostentatious of the hotels are the luxury giants. These elegant edifices seem more like millionaires' playrooms than sleeping accommodations. When travelers walk into the lobby, they wonder if they are on a movie set. Expensive furniture, rugs, plants of all varieties can be seen everywhere. The employees are immaculately dressed in formal clothing, and they are attentive to one's every concern. Usually these hotels have a variety of services to offer—cocktail bars, lounges, pools, a first-class restaurant with international chefs. The people who stay in these hotels are often celebrities from the film industries, politicians, business people from large multinational corporations, or wealthy individuals on vacation. Not for the ordinary traveler, these hotels are tourist attractions in their own right.

The international chains are the next level of hotel one sees around the world. While very nice, and quite expensive also, they lack the class, the age, and the reputation of the luxury hotels. The decor and design of these first-class hotel chains are quite attractive—the furniture is lovely, the lobbies and restaurants are luxurious. Nevertheless, though the travelers know they are in good hotels, they also know there is a higher level. The employees are courteous and offer good service, but they do not cater to the guest's every whim. Usually these hotels are filled with upper-class tourists and well-to-do business people.

A third type of hotel one can find when traveling is the standard family lodging place. These are often listed as budget hotels. The lobby is comfortable, but it lacks the space and the extra touches of the fancier hotels. There will be couches, chairs, perhaps a television, but the area is not meant for many people. Sometimes there is a coffee shop or snack bar connected to the lobby, but it will not offer anything extraordinary—just regular food and service. Employees of these hotels are often friendly, but they do not treat people as lords or masters, just as ordinary people who are temporary guests of the hotel.

The final class of hotel one can stay at is the bare bones "hole-in-the-wall." Most of these hotels are quite small and tucked away on a narrow street in an obscure part of town. Often there is no lobby to speak of—just a walkway to the front desk where the traveler pays for a room before getting a key. The only employee is the desk clerk, and he or she is probably not that friendly. If hungry, the traveler has to find a shop or a food stall down the street. Not meant for the ordinary middle-class traveler, these hotels are for people with little money or for people who do not much care where they sleep.

An interesting observation about these hotels is that they always seem to do good business. Either certain travelers gravitate to specific types of hotels or the hotels were built to attract different levels of travelers. In any event, whatever one's style of living or financial condition, one can probably find a hotel to satisfy.

ASSIGNMENT

For each of the following classification essay topics that you choose or are assigned, follow these steps:

1. Explore the topic with one of the invention exercises described in Chapter 1.
2. After examining the information gathered through the invention activities, formulate a thesis statement (include the basis of classification).
3. Determine the name and number of classes you are going to discuss.
4. Identify an audience for your paper.
5. Write a first draft, making sure that you have not included too many or too few classes. Have all members of the set been assigned to a class? (Also pay attention to all of the other elements of the essay: the opening paragraph, the body paragraphs, the closing paragraph, and the title.)
6. Wait at least one day, then go over your first draft, revising it for organization, deletions, and additions.

7. Write the second draft of the essay. Make sure you edit the draft before you turn it in.

Suggested Writing Topics

- Types of courage
- Foreigners living in your country
- Personality types in your family
- Communication styles
- Interactions among nations

Cause or Effect

Suppose you had an automobile accident with your parents' car and you were trying to explain to them why the accident happened. They in turn tell you what will happen as a result of the accident. In this case, you are using *cause* and your parents are using *effect* to discuss the incident. Cause and effect, although obviously related, are two separate ways of viewing an event.

A *cause* paper presents the reasons why an event happened. Most events result from a number of causes, which do not necessarily have to be related to each other. For example, your car accident might have been the result of a wet road, a loud radio, and your slow braking reaction. All of these causes worked together to create the accident; one cause did not relate directly to another. In writing a paper based on causes, you should distinguish between the contributing causes (e.g., the wet road) and the things that simply happened before the event. Eating chicken for lunch, for instance, might have happened immediately before the accident but it probably did not cause it. Interpreting a previous activity as a cause is a common mistake for many writers. Be careful not to confuse the two.

In a cause paper, develop only those causes that are closely related in time to the event. The appropriate time relationship of an event and its causes depends upon the magnitude and complexity of that event. For a historical event, you might cite causes occurring a few years or even decades before the event you are writing about, but you would not want to include events that happened centuries ago. For example, if you were discussing the causes of Adolf Hitler's 1933 election to Chancellor, one of the causes could be the condition of Germany immediately after World War I (a dozen years earlier). For your automobile accident, however, you would not want to cite as a cause something that happened twelve years earlier.

Also beware of *false* causal relationships. An example is your learning to read in school: even though you were probably sitting at a desk, it would be absurd to say that sitting at a desk was one of the causes for your learning to read. Most of the time a false cause-effect relationship is not as absurd as this example, so you have to be careful when choosing causes.

An *effect* paper presents the effects or results of a particular occurrence. The effects should be distinct and separate from one another; they should not develop out of each other. Furthermore, the effects should not be too distant in time. Just as you should focus on causes closely related in time, discuss only those effects that are closely related in time to your event.

In your thesis statement, you should make it clear to your reader whether the paper is being developed by *cause* or by *effect*. If your thesis presents a cause statement, your body paragraphs should discuss the cause relationships. See the following example.

CAUSE

Thesis: In retrospect, many factors contributed to the accident I had last week.
1. Wet road
2. Loud radio (distraction)
3. Slow braking reaction

If, on the other hand, your thesis presents an effect statement, your body paragraphs should discuss effects. See the following example.

EFFECT

Thesis: I noticed several changes in my life as a result of my car accident.
1. Car insurance rates went up
2. Spent money on repairs and police fine
3. Lost use of car while it was being repaired

Notice that each of the foregoing examples presents the same accident from two different viewpoints—the first as cause, the second as effect. Do not mix the two in the body of any one essay.

Although most cause or effect papers deal with events, you can also use this strategy of development to discuss the reasons for or the results of a condition or state (such as being in debt, being overweight, being in love, possessing a particular personality trait). If you discuss a condition or state, the same guidelines as those for discussing an event apply.

Points to Remember
- Frame your thesis as a clear statement of either cause *or* effect.
- Be sure your causes or effects are distinct and separate.
- Include only contributing factors in cause papers.
- Discuss only those causes or effects closely related in time to the event.
- Distinguish between actual and false causes and effects before you start writing.

SAMPLE CAUSE OR EFFECT ESSAY:

Gateway to the World

The various traditions of education have always placed an importance on the learning of other languages, though the motives have often varied. Knowing a second or third language was supposed to round out an individual's personal education, just as knowledge of science or the arts did. Regardless of any theoretical value, however, there are many practical reasons students of any nation should learn foreign languages. The knowledge of even one more language has distinct effects on an individual.

One effect of knowing a second language is that a person can experience first hand the great literature of another people. One can read the *Shah Nameh* in Persian, *Candide* in French, *El Cid* in Spanish, or the *Tales of Genji* in Japanese. No longer is someone without knowledge of language *X* forced to read translations in his or her native language. Instead, one can experience directly the power and the subtleties of the original, which are often lost in translations. One can feel the flow of the language, the combinations of sounds and word order, all of which combine to bring the work alive—alive as the artist intentionally planned.

The ability to read in another language reinforces a second effect: the gaining of knowledge about another culture. Through reading and speaking a second language, one can gain insight into the fabric that enfolds the life of another culture. Translations are screens that hide the complexity of the lives of other cultures. When one learns a second language, one sees that there are other ways of eating, working, or relating to those around one. Learning that "I missed the bus" would be *"Se me paso el autobus"* (the bus passed me by) in Spanish clearly demonstrates that there are alternative ways to see how men relate to the environment. In English, man has the responsibility as an actor in the world around him. In Spanish, man is only one actor among many and his responsibility is different than in English. Even such commonplace items as food become exciting as we learn of them in another language. The variety of different foods, the manner of eating them, and the land in which they are grown are all part of the culture of another people and their language. When we learn this language, we necessarily learn about this culture.

Perhaps the most powerful effect of learning another language is communication. With a second—or third or fourth—language, one can make contact with a fellow human being. All too often we see ourselves divided from our brothers and sisters by notions of nationality, race, or religion. Language is one more barrier that separates humans. If we overcome that barrier by learning other languages, we can experience our common humanity; no longer are we isolated from each other. With communication, we see that the joys and fears of all people are the same. Everyone is human, with all the attendant strengths and weaknesses. No greater good could happen than that the people of the world understand each other.

Many people study foreign languages because of a school requirement. Others learn a second language because of more practical reasons. Regardless of the reasons for acquiring a new language, however, the effects are considerable. Since greater understanding and communication with other cultures and people are two important by-products, we all would do well if we studied at least one more language. In this way, we could contribute one small part to the achieving of world peace.

ASSIGNMENT

For each of the cause or effect essay topics that you choose or are assigned, follow these steps:

1. Explore the topic with one of the invention exercises described in Chapter 1.
2. After examining the information gathered through the invention activities, formulate a thesis statement that clearly indicates whether your paper is about causes or effects.
3. Identify an audience for your paper.
4. Determine the actual causes or effects you will be discussing in your paper.
5. Write a first draft, making sure that your causes or effects are appropriate: separate, contributing, actual, and closely related in time to the event. (Also pay attention to all of the other elements of the essay: the opening paragraph, the body paragraphs, the closing paragraph, and the title.)
6. Wait at least one day, then go over your first draft, revising it for reorganization, deletions, and additions.
7. Write the second draft of the essay. Make sure you edit the draft before you turn it in.

Suggested Writing Topics

- A person's possessing a good sense of humor
- The existence of prejudice in a community
- A natural phenomenon (a hurricane, earthquake, tidal wave, snowstorm, and so on)
- A broken relationship
- A change in a national tradition (specify the tradition and the country)

Process

The process paper instructs or explains. It can instruct the reader how to do something, such as how to write a computer program. It can also explain how something happened or how something works, such as how Australia was colonized or how a nuclear reaction occurs. Thus, there are two types of process essays: *instructional* and *explanatory.*

All process papers should be developed in chronological order. Because you are writing about something that happens or happened over time, make sure that you do not jump ahead or backwards in time. Present events and actions as they naturally occur. It is easy to see the necessity for chronological order if you imagine trying to follow a set of directions that are not in order. You would only become confused or frustrated.

Choose a subject that is limited so that you can present the process in detail. You could not give complete information on how to build a house in a process essay because there is too much to write about. You could, however, tell your reader how to build a fireplace, hang a door, or lay tile.

To present your information clearly in an instructional paper, you should break down the process. With a process that does not involve too many steps, such as boiling an egg, this is easy. Be careful, however, to include each step in the process. Do not leave out any step or your reader will not be able to achieve the desired results. For a more complicated process, it is helpful to first list the *major* steps. These major steps are then broken down into individual steps. The following outline shows the major steps of repotting a plant.

HOW TO REPOT A HOUSE PLANT

Thesis: Anyone who keeps plants around the house should know the procedure involved in repotting a plant.

  I. Preparation
 II. Depotting from original pot
III. Repotting into new pot
 IV. Postpotting care

The breaking down of an instructional process into major steps and individual steps prevents the reader from getting lost in the process. This can be seen clearly in the next outline on developing slide film. Grouping the nineteen individual steps into three major steps makes the process much easier to follow and to understand.

DEVELOPING SLIDE FILM AT HOME

Thesis: Once the proper technique is known, amateur photographers can easily process their own slide film at home.

  I. Preparation
    A. Gather all equipment (list)
    B. Remove film from canister
    C. Load on reel
    D. Place in film tank
 II. Processing
    A. First developer
    B. Water rinse

    C. Reversal bath
    D. Color developer
    E. Stop bath
    F. Water rinse
    G. Bleach
    H. Fixer
    I. Water rinse
    J. Stabilizer
    K. Dry
III. Mounting
    A. Cut film
    B. Place in mount
    C. Seal
    D. Label

When writing about a process that requires particular tools or equipment, list these items before you begin giving instructions. Preparing slide film for processing, for instance, requires having film, a film tank and lid, a film reel, a pair of scissors, a bottle opener, and a changing bag or a darkroom. Be sure to tell your reader this before giving instructions to mix the chemicals for processing. Also, present each step simply and directly. Put yourself in your reader's place and imagine trying to follow the instructions. After all, the whole purpose of an instructional process paper is to tell your readers how to do something; after your readers have read your paper, *they* should be able to do the activity.

An *explanatory* process essay explains how a particular event occurred or gives information on how an action occurs or how an object works. An explanatory paper provides a broad overview of the subject to the reader, not a detailed description of an activity.

The steps of your explanatory process will differ from the steps in an instructional process. First of all, an explanatory process highlights only the most important steps of the entire process. You give the readers enough information about each step to increase their knowledge and understanding of the process as a whole; however, the minute details describing an instructional process would probably be omitted. When describing slide film processing (instructional), you need to include all the steps in detail, but if you were to explain how a ballet is put on stage (explanatory), you would discuss only the most relevant steps. As you can see from the following example, the reader still gains a comprehensive understanding of the process:

HOW A BALLET IS PUT ON STAGE

Thesis: Anyone who has ever marveled at the beauty of a professional ballet performance will appreciate knowing all the work that goes into its preparation.

I. Program Planning
    A. Deciding on:

      1. ballet
      2. music
      3. choreography
   B. Selecting soloists and principles
   C. Choosing company
  II. Rehearsing
   A. Practicing individual parts
   B. Practicing entire ballet
   C. Practicing with orchestra
 III. Staging
   A. Designing and fitting costumes
   B. Rehearsing with:
      1. technical crews
      2. sets
      3. props
      4. lighting

Remember that the reader is not going to be recreating the activity described in an explanatory process. Nevertheless, although you do not have to provide detailed information on the major steps of the process, be sure you do not leave out any information necessary to the general understanding of the process.

Points to Remember

- State your thesis so that it indicates whether your paper is instructional or explanatory.
- Keep to a strict chronological order.
- Group individual steps into major steps, if appropriate.
- In an instructional paper, include all necessary steps, present details thoroughly (list tools and equipment), keep directions short and simple.
- In an explanatory paper, discuss only the most significant steps within each major step.

SAMPLE PROCESS ESSAY:

Homeward Bound

Most college students concern themselves with getting good grades. This makes a great deal of sense because many benefits are realized: academic honors, pride, good jobs. Some students, however, understand that college is not vital to one's career and regret their decision to enroll. Life would be much easier, after all, watching television all day and partying all night. But once they have made the mistake of applying for admission, they see no way out of four more years of school. If you are one of these students, with a little planning, you too can be free of college forever. Flunking out of college is actually a simple procedure if you go about it in the correct manner.

The first obstacle to overcome is registration. Prospective flunk-outs should be sure to pick the hardest courses possible. Instead of taking an introductory class in mathematics, you should register for an upper-level course, like Differential Equations or Topological Theory. The lower-level courses might be too easy to pass. And why take Basic if it is possible to enroll in Assembly Language in computer science? Business Law is another good class— lots of reading and difficult concepts to master. Picking good courses like these start you off with a great opportunity to earn a low grade point average.

After arranging a good schedule, you need to think of the next few days. The first few days in a class are vital to any student on the road to failure. On these days, be sure to arrive to class late, twenty or thirty minutes late. Skipping the first class or two is sometimes an even better alternative. That way all the course requirements and first assignments are missed. This then gives you the opportunity to ask the teacher questions he or she has already explained. And do not bring textbooks or other material to class. Always look unprepared and as if you want to be somewhere else. You have to be sure, however, that the professors know your name; otherwise, when grading comes around, they will not be able to remember that you are the student in the back row, taking up space and holding up the wall.

The next step in flunking out deals with homework and tests. Never—repeat, never—turn in homework on time. Turn it in a day or two late, and complain about the assignment at the same time. Often it might be useful to give excuses—like your other classes required work, or you forgot, or you had to visit a friend in another city. Remember, also, to do the homework wrong. If your work is good, the teacher might overlook your other faults. Tests are a relatively simple matter. Don't study. Miss one or two exams. Write question marks in the space for answers. Write a math equation on a history test and an important date on a math test. You can always say that you did not understand the question or that the test was too hard. Whether for homework or for a test, try to keep your score below 50 percent.

The final step to getting kicked out of school is probably the easiest—blow the final exam. In some ways this step is an elaboration on the semester tests, but the finals are much more important. If you do well on a final, you might pass the course anyway, so be careful. You could miss the final for a course, but if the professor is kind, a make-up might be offered to you. The best bet is to show up and work hard at failing. Then you can be assured of the outcome. Many of the questions you will not have to worry about because by this time you will have no idea of the answers. But if you do know an answer by accident, be sure to write something else. And don't finish the exam. Leave at least a couple of questions unanswered and turn it in early. Mention your name, or point to it on the exam and casually say something like, "I really need an *A* in this course because I'm flunking all my other ones. And this course isn't in my major anyway." You can be assured that the instructor will be impressed and remember you when the final grades are recorded.

All in all, flunking out of college isn't too difficult, but you do have to pay attention to how you go about it. With a little forethought and planning, even the smartest student can receive a 0.00 GPA. And while you're packing your bags to go home, enjoy the thought of what awaits you. . . .

ASSIGNMENT

For each of the following process essay topics that you choose or are assigned, follow these steps:

1. Explore the topic with one of the invention exercises described in Chapter 1.
2. After examining the information gathered through the invention activities, formulate a thesis statement that reflects an instructional or explanatory process.
3. Identify an audience for your paper.
4. Divide the process into chronological steps. Group the individual steps into major steps if necessary.
5. Write a first draft of the paper. (Pay attention to all the other elements of the essay: the opening paragraph, the body paragraphs, the closing paragraph, and the title.)
6. Wait at least one day, then go over your first draft, revising it for organization, deletions, and additions.
7. Write the second draft of the essay. Make sure you edit the draft before you turn it in.

Suggested Writing Topics

- Describe how to do a chore you were responsible for as a child.
- Describe how a technical device (telephone, camera, computer) works.
- Describe how *not* to have fun at a party.
- Describe how a major holiday is celebrated in your family.
- Describe how a major historical event occurred.

Extended Definition

Extended definition is used to clarify concepts or objects. For example, it can be used to explain the abstract notions of *justice* or *beauty*. Extended definition also can allow the business student to explain the meaning of *inflation* on a test; the English teacher to explain the *present perfect* to students; and the chemist to explain *oxidation* to a reporter.

To develop a paper using extended definition, you begin by identifying the class to which your subject belongs. For example, you could begin an essay defining Briards by stating that the Briard belongs to the class of sheepdogs. The remainder of the body of your paper would focus on distinguishing and describing those specific features, characteristics, or components of your subject that set it apart from the rest of the items in the same class. In the case of the Briard, the dog is distinguished from other sheepdogs by its origin, appearance, temperament, and abilities.

You can also make use of some of the other strategies already discussed in this chapter. You can clarify your subject by comparing or contrasting it to synonymous and antonymous subjects; you can give examples of how the term is used, or you can explain how the term was developed and came to its present meaning. This last technique works particularly well with slang, technical terminology, and political expressions.

Consider the following ways in which *terrorism* can be defined:

class:—political actions
features:—motive
        adversaries
        victims
        unexpected attack
        death/destruction
contrast:—war
comparison:—murder
example:—1972 Munich Olympics: raid on Israeli team
        1983 bombing of South Korean officials in Burma
        Irish Republican Army bombings in London
history:—first use of term
        growing use
        term used daily in media

Writing circular definitions and relying on dictionary definitions are two pitfalls to avoid when writing extended definition papers. Circular definitions are created by using, within the definition itself, a variation of the word you are trying to define. For example, if you are writing a paper defining a *conservative*, do not write that a conservative is a person with conservative ideas. Obviously, this statement does not contribute any information or understanding about what a conservative is. Similarly, avoid using a definition from a dictionary as part of your own definition—your readers can look up this definition themselves. Instead, you should give a more comprehensive understanding of your subject—you should give an *extended* definition.

Points to Remember
- Define only concepts or objects that need clarification: those that are abstract, unfamiliar, complex, or technical.
- Identify the class and discuss the distinguishing features of your concept or object.

- To extend your definition, include a variety of strategies in the body paragraphs.
- Beware of circular and dictionary definitions.

SAMPLE EXTENDED DEFINITION ESSAY:

The True Artist

When we hear the word "artist," probably one of the first images that comes to mind is that of a person with an easel and paintbrush recreating his or her surroundings on canvas. The painter, however, is only one example of an artist. Poets, sculptors, and musicians are also artists in that they practice one of the fine arts (music, dance, poetry, sculpture, and the graphic arts). Some might even go so far as to envision artists as unconventional, temperamental individuals whose single-minded preoccupation with finishing a sonata or writing an epic poem makes them oblivious to the typical concerns of society. While these characteristics may be true of some artists, they actually stereotype artists rather than give us a very accurate understanding of what an artist is. In truth, being an artist is not dependent on a person's profession or personality. Artists, whether painters or physicists, are people who have the technical expertise in their chosen fields, who use creatively the material in the world around them, and who have the urge to communicate something relevant about human beings.

Artists are frequently confused with artisans or craftsmen. Artisans and craftsmen produce objects from raw materials, objects which are often beautiful. But many of the objects are utilitarian in nature; they are not created for the sake of beauty alone. In this sense, artisans and craftsmen are simply manufacturers. In addition, craftsmen and artisans usually lack the creative vision innate to the artist. Craftsmen follow designs; artists search for meanings, interpretations.

Several characteristics identify artists. First, artists are masters of the tools and materials of their art. They must persevere in practicing their trades, often spending many years as apprentices or students. In this way, artists may be confused with craftsmen. Craftsmen must also develop technical skill to practice their trades or handicrafts. Artists, however, use their technical skills to impart a spiritual or visionary element to their work. In the dramatic monologue, "Andrea del Sarto," Robert Browning distinguishes between Andrea del Sarto, the faultless painter, and Michelangelo, a "real" artist. Andrea del Sarto can reproduce reality flawlessly, but his work is flat and uninspired; his "reach" will never "exceed his grasp." An artist, suggests Browning, is not someone with just the talent to recreate the material world in another medium, but someone who can transform that world according to his or her own vision and understanding. The creation of a work of art, then, is an act of discovery, not of replication. Another poet, William Blake, in his work "The Tyger," states that the artist must possess both the "hand" (ability) and the "eye" (vision) to create.

This leads to another attribute of an artist. In addition to being a skilled technician with a vision to impart, the artist is also experimental and creative in the use of raw materials. This is what separates artists from most people. While they still make use of the materials of the commonplace world, they look at these materials from a fresh angle. Artists rearrange these materials to present us with something new, delightful, or thought-provoking. An example of this is seen readily in Picasso's sculpture of a bull's head. It usually takes the onlooker by surprise that the artist has fashioned this beast out of an ordinary bicycle seat and handlebars.

Finally, besides having the technical ability and creative insight to translate reality into an imaginative experience, artists have an urge to communicate their perceptions about human relationships and human nature to an audience. The artist's work functions much as a mirror for expressing a unique understanding of how people live. Sometimes, as in the case of Diego Rivera, whose murals adorn the walls of numerous federal buildings and schools in Mexico City, artists may express themselves directly. The same is true of Wagner, who used musical "motifs" to represent certain characters in his operas. In both cases, the works of these two artists present stories that show how human beings live and relate to each other. Often, however, artists communicate in symbols.

Examples of true artists are found easily. They may be recognized artists such as Picasso (a Spanish painter and sculptor) or Basho (a Japanese poet). But an artist may also be the neighbor who takes photographs or the student dancing at a disco on weekends. If one combines technical skill with a vision, creates the extraordinary out of the ordinary, and communicates the reality of human existence to others, we can properly say that this person is an artist.

Although people may disagree on whether they like a particular piece of art, they should all be able to recognize if someone is an artist or not. The quality of art may be determined by one's preferences; the recognition of an artist, however, should be the same for all. We should remember that an artist does not dress in one particular fashion, or live in a certain part of town—the person sitting next to us on a bus is an artist if he or she possesses the proper characteristics.

ASSIGNMENT

For each of the following extended definition essay topics that you choose or are assigned, follow these steps:

1. Explore the topic with one of the invention exercises described in Chapter 1.
2. After examining the information gathered through invention activities, formulate a thesis statement that indicates you will be defining a concept or object.
3. Identify an audience for your paper.
4. Determine some of the possible ways to define your topic (including class, distinguishing features, and other appropriate strategies).
5. Write a first draft. (Pay attention to all of the other elements of the essay: the opening paragraph, the body paragraphs, the closing paragraph, and the title.)
6. Wait at least one day, then go over your first draft, revising it for reorganization, deletions, and additions.
7. Write the second draft of the essay. Make sure you edit the draft before you turn it in.

Suggested Writing Topics

- A patriot/patriotism
- A nonconformist/nonconformity
- A friend/friendship
- A successful person/success
- A slang word, a technical term, or an abstract concept of your choice

Editing

The final step in the writing process is editing. Keep in mind that revising and editing are two different activities. When you revise, you make changes in *what* you write; when you edit, you correct *how* you wrote something. Revision improves the content and the organization of your material. Editing, on the other hand, polishes the surface features of writing, such as grammar, punctuation, and mechanics. You might think of this as similar to a job interview. An applicant's background and knowledge are analagous to the content of a paper, whereas the appearance at the interview—the applicant's clothing and grooming—are the surface features. Just as for the job applicant, both your paper's content and appearance are important to making a favorable impression on your audience.

GRAMMAR

All languages have grammar rules, but the rules differ from language to language. As a student whose first language is not English, you need to be especially attentive to English grammar when writing. You should also remember that writing is different from speaking. Spoken language is rapid and temporary; written language is relatively permanent and often requires time for understanding. Written language is also more elaborate—ideas can be quite complex. The writer-reader relationship provides the freedom to expand and develop many aspects of a topic. Nevertheless, the writing-reading situation is a structured operation governed by fairly strict rules. Although grammar in speech need not be perfect in order for you to be understood, the formality of writing demands close adherence to the conventions of written English. This section presents aspects of grammar that cause the most problems for writers.

Fragments

A simple declarative sentence consists of at least two words, a subject and a verb, which, when combined, state a complete thought:

Dogs   bark.
(subject)   (verb)

Sentence fragments may appear to be simple sentences, but as the word *fragment* implies, at least one of the basic components of a simple sentence is missing, i.e., either the subject or the verb is omitted. Every sentence in English (except for commands) needs a subject. Similarly, each sentence in English needs a complete verb. You can usually correct a fragment in several ways, as demonstrated below:

Fragment: I like to visit the railroad station. *To watch all the trains leaving for distant destinations.*

Revised: I like to visit the railroad station to watch all the trains leaving for distant destinations.

Revised: I like to visit the railroad station. To watch all the the trains leaving for distant destinations is exciting.

Revised: I like to visit the railroad station. I enjoy watching all the trains leaving for distant destinations.

Run-on Sentences

Two or more independent clauses or complete sentences must be connected by a comma and a coordinating conjunction or separated by other punctuation (semicolon or period). This lets your reader know where one grammatical thought stops and another begins. Do not run together two independent clauses without the appropriate punctuation.

Run-On: I love horseback riding the feeling of freedom surpasses any other sensation.

Revised: I love horseback riding; the feeling of freedom surpasses any other sensation.

Revised: I love horseback riding, for the feeling of freedom surpasses any other sensation.

Revised: I love horseback riding. The feeling of freedom surpasses any other sensation.

Comma Splices

If you connect two or more independent clauses with punctuation, you should not do it with a comma alone. Because both of your sentences are independent clauses, they must be marked by punctuation that indicates the relationship between the two complete thoughts: either a comma and a coordinating conjunction, a semicolon, or a period. Be careful. Many students use commas when they really should be using other punctuation.

Comma Splice: The tourists went to the outdoor market, they bought several of the tropical flowers offered for sale.
Revised: The tourists went to the outdoor market. They bought several of the tropical flowers offered for sale.
Revised: The tourists went to the outdoor market, and they bought several of the tropical flowers offered for sale.
Revised: The tourists went to the outdoor market; they bought several of the tropical flowers offered for sale.

Subject–Verb Agreement

Be sure that your subject and verb agree in number (singular or plural). In English, there are two instances in which you have to be especially careful of subject–verb agreement. The first is with a compound subject (two subjects joined by *and*). Whether these two individual subjects are singular, plural, or mixed, as a unit they are plural. Thus the verb should always be plural.

The dog and the cat (compound subject)   play (plural verb)   together.

The second problematic instance is when the subject units are linked by *either . . . or* or *neither . . . nor.* In this case, the verb should agree with the subject closest to it.

Either my dog or the neighbor's cats (2nd subject plural)   have eaten (plural verb)   my grilled steak.

Neither my dogs nor the neigbor's cat (2nd subject singular)   likes (singular verb)   the rain.

Noun–Pronoun Agreement

Agreement between nouns and pronouns usually does not create difficulties; however, certain words such as *each, neither, everyone, everybody, no one,* and *nobody* often present problems. Although they seem to have a plural meaning, words ending in *one* or *body* are singular. Therefore, their pronouns should be singular also.

Problem: Everybody planning to major in business is advised to take accounting courses during *their* first two years of study.
Revised: Everybody planning to major in business is advised to take

accounting courses during *his or her* first two years of study.

Problem: Nobody is willing to offer *their* opinion in Professor Grey's classes.

Revised: Nobody is willing to offer *his or her* opinion in Professor Grey's classes.

Dependent Clauses

Complex sentences are made up of one independent clause and one or more dependent clauses. Although independent clauses can stand alone as a sentence, dependent clauses cannot. Dependent clauses are easy to identify—although a dependent clause contains a subject and a verb, it begins with a word like *who, where, that, although, since, because, if,* and *after.* There are three types of dependent clauses: noun clauses, adjective clauses, and adverb clauses.

Noun Clauses

A noun clause contains a subject and a verb, but the whole clause is considered one complete unit. The noun clause may be used in place of a noun as a subject, object, or object of a preposition. Noun clauses typically begin with a question word *(who, what, where, when, why, how), whether* or *if,* or *that.*

> *Whoever reads the textbook carefully* will certainly pass the test.
> There is no way of knowing *whether he will come or not.*
> We do not know *what we will eat for dinner.*
> I am not sure *if he will come.*
> Why did he say *that I should not bother him?*
> Tell them *that I cannot come today.*
> *Where they are going to sleep* is a mystery to me.
> They have no interest in *what the speaker is saying.*
> She told me *when she was going to leave,* but I forgot.
> I wish I knew *why tests are always so hard.*
> You will learn *how you can do differential equations in the math class.*

Adjective Clauses

An adjective clause (also called a relative clause) is a dependent clause that modifies a noun or pronoun. It also can modify a subject or object, as well as the object of a preposition. Adjective clauses begin with the word *who/whom, which, that, whose, where,* or *when.*

> The man *who called me* is a friend of my brother.
> I never met the person *whom I telephoned.*
> Buy the required textbook, *which can be found in the bookstore.*
> The building *that the terrorists blew up* housed thirty-seven people.

I would like to know the person *whose car is parked behind mine.*
The time *when a person should study* depends on the individual's characteristics.
We never found out the place *where we were to meet.*
Early morning is the time *when I feel most alive.*

Sometimes use commas to set off adjective clauses (it all depends upon the meaning to be conveyed). For a further discussion, refer to the comma rules in the punctuation section of this chapter.

Adverb Clauses

An adverb clause is a dependent clause that modifies a verb, adjective, or adverb. Adverb clauses are used to show relationships of time, cause and effect, opposition, and condition.

After we saw the show, we went out dancing.
They will work on the project *when they have finished the paper.*
Since he never said his name, I don't know who he is.
We will wait for them *until the class begins.*
Because I had a poor grade on the first test, I studied twice as hard before the second test.
The professor always has time for his students *even though he teaches four classes.*
Unless the weather warms up soon, I think I will go crazy.
They plan to go skating *if the lake is frozen tomorrow.*

When the dependent clause follows the independent clause, you do not use punctuation. However, when the dependent clause *precedes* the independent clause, separate them by a comma to show that the normal order of the sentence is inverted.

Dangling Modifiers

Introductory modifiers that are meant to refer to the subject of the sentence but that grammatically do not are called *dangling modifiers*. Look at the following sentence:

Dangling: Fearful of losing something valuable in the airplane, the luggage went under his seat.

Because introductory modifiers must refer to the subject of a sentence, in this sentence the *luggage* is incorrectly being described as fearful. Obviously this cannot be the case. The writer actually meant to say that the *person* who owned the luggage was fearful. This sentence must therefore be revised to make a person the subject of the sentence. See the following revision:

> Revised: Fearful of losing something valuable in the airplane, he placed his luggage under his seat.

If you use an introductory modifier, make sure that you use a proper subject for the sentence.

Alternatively, you could turn the introductory modifier into a subordinate clause, as illustrated in the next example:

> Dangling: After reading the minutes of the previous meeting, a heated discussion among the managers began.
> Revised: After the secretary read the minutes of the previous meeting, a heated discussion among the managers began.

Here are other examples of dangling modifiers:

> Dangling Participle: Arriving early, the party had not yet started.
> Revised: Arriving early, we realized that the party had not yet started.
> Dangling Gerund: After dancing for several hours, the chairs looked inviting.
> Revised: After dancing for several hours, we thought the chairs looked inviting.
> Dangling Infinitive: To speak a language fluently, much practice is necessary.
> Revised: To speak a language fluently, a person needs much practice.
> Dangling Elliptical Clause: When only eight years old, my family took a trip around the world.
> Revised: When only eight years old, I traveled around the world with my family.

Parallelism

If a sentence contains elements joined by coordinating conjunctions, these elements must be parallel in form. In other words, all of the elements should be nouns, or adjectives, or infinitive phrases, or prepositional phrases. Do not mix structures.

> Nonparallel: I bought that make of car for its reliability, it is durable, and it cost little.
> Parallel: I bought that make of car for its reliability, durability, and economy.
> Parallel: I bought that make of car because it was reliable, durable, and economical.
> Parallel: I bought that make of car because it always worked, it stood up to hard use, and it used little gas.

As with coordinating conjunctions, if you are joining elements using correlative conjunctions (*either . . . or, not only . . . but also*), each element must be expressed in the same grammatical form.

Professor Green teaches both *computer science* and *English*.
We not only *saw the movie* but also *read the book*.
I plan either *to stay home* or *to visit friends*.
Neither *studying for the test* nor *cleaning my room* interests me.

Tense Shift

Maintain consistent verb tenses in a sentence. Do not shift from one time frame to another. In most sentences, each verb should have the same tense form.

Shift: When our club *visited* New York City, we all *go* to the Museum of Modern Art.
Revised: When our club *visits* New York City, we all *go* to the Museum of Modern Art.
Shift: After I *finished* reading the book, I *am playing* basketball.
Revised: After I *finished* reading the book, I *played* basketball.

Person/Number Shift

Maintain a consistent point of view for person and number. Do not shift your perspective from one person to another or from singular to plural.

Shift: When *you* travel, *he or she* should carry a small first-aid kit.
Revised: When a *person* travels, *he or she* should carry a small first-aid kit.
Revised: When *you* travel, *you* should carry a small first-aid kit.
Shift: *Students* may be referred to counseling by *his or her* teachers, advisors, or parents.
Revised: *A student may be referred to counseling by his or her* teachers, advisors, or parents.
Revised: *Students* may be referred to counseling by *their* teachers, advisors, or parents.

Voice Shift

Maintain one voice (either active or passive) within a single sentence.

Shift: The clerk dreams of being a manager someday, but her dreams are not acted upon.
Revised: The clerk dreams of being a manager someday, but she does not act upon her dreams.

Note: Generally, it is preferable to write in the active voice. The active voice is usually clearer and more straightforward. If you use the passive voice, be sure that you have a reason, e.g., the subject is unimportant or unknown.

PUNCTUATION

Using punctuation correctly when you write in English is very important. Mistakes in punctuation are noticed very quickly by experienced readers and writers. Because punctuation is so noticeable, a few mistakes can outweigh good elements of your essay (i.e., your interesting content and effective organization can be overlooked by someone who is bothered by punctuation problems). Punctuation is important because it helps show how ideas are linked together. The period, comma, or semicolon, for example, all have different significance, and if they are used incorrectly (or omitted when they should be used), the reader may become confused about what you are trying to say.

One cautionary note: Punctuation rules are fairly rigid and exact. Do not rely on "feel" to decide whether or not to use a punctuation mark. Especially do not rely on speech patterns (e.g., do not use commas in a sentence at the place where you would pause when speaking). Remember that speech and writing use two different sets of rules and procedures. Whenever you use a punctuation mark, have a reason for it—the best reason is a rule. If you do not know a rule or cannot find a rule in one of your English books, do not use the punctuation mark. If in doubt, you are probably wiser not to use it at that particular spot.

The Period

Use a period at the end of declarative or imperative sentences.

> The class starts at 11:30.
> Always turn in your assignments on time.

Use a period with initials and with most abbreviations. Do not use periods with abbreviations of organizations or government agencies (e.g., NATO, OPEC, ASEAN).

> J. R. Ewing
> John F. Kennedy
> Dr.
> Mr.
> etc.
> U.S.A.

The Question Mark

Use a question mark at the end of a direct question.

When will you be leaving for Brazil?
Are you sure that Sam is coming today?

Do not use a question mark after an indirect question.

They asked me when I would leave.

The Exclamation Mark

Use an exclamation mark to indicate strong feeling or emphasis.

Hey! What are you doing to my car!
If we don't stop the nuclear arms race, we will all die!

The Comma

Use a comma to separate two independent clauses joined by a coordinating conjunction (*and, but, or, nor, for, yet*). The comma comes before the coordinating conjunction.

I wanted to tell him the truth, but I did not want to hurt him.
College is a time for learning, yet it is also a time for enjoyment.
She knew what she had to do to pass the course, and she organized her schedule accordingly.

DO NOT separate two sentences with a comma only. This is a comma splice.
DO NOT use a comma to separate two words or phrases joined by a coordinating conjunction. To use a comma with a coordinating conjunction, each element of the pair has to be an independent clause.
Use a single comma to set off introductory words, phrases, or clauses (any material that comes before the subject of the independent clause).

Nevertheless, the government still thinks this should be done.
In the morning, the world seems a place full of hope and beauty.
If you study the material, you should not have any trouble taking the exam.

Be careful not to let a single comma separate a subject and its verb.
Use two commas to set off interrupting or nonessential material in the middle of the sentence. If the material can be deleted or moved elsewhere in the sentence, it probably needs two commas.

The new governor, fortunately, started making changes immediately.
The monthly report, written by our new salesman, should have already reached you.
I will, of course, help you as much as I can.

Enclosing words in the middle of a sentence with two commas indicates that these words can be deleted with no loss of meaning to the sentence. If the material is necessary to understand the full meaning of the sentence, do not enclose it with commas. Look at the following two sentences:

> Bill's sister, who lives in Chicago, arrived on the midnight flight. (This sentence tells the reader that Bill has only one sister, and she lives in Chicago. You can remove the words *who lives in Chicago* and the sentence meaning is not obscured. Therefore, you should use commas here.)
> Bill's sister who lives in Chicago arrived on the midnight flight. (This sentence tells the reader that Bill has several sisters, and only one lives in Chicago. If you deleted the words *who lives in Chicago,* the reader would not know which sister arrived. Therefore, you should not use commas here.)

Use a single comma to set off material that follows the independent clause and which explains, amplifies, or offers a contrast to it.

> Helen was chosen to lead the procession, not Christine.
> Electrical power throughout the city failed, causing numerous emergencies.

Use a single comma to set off nonessential material that modifies the last element of a sentence. If the material can be deleted without affecting the meaning of the sentence, it is nonessential.

> We all ran toward the bridge, which was about to collapse.
> The truck nearly ran over Uncle Joe, who was extremely angry at such bad driving.
> They all clapped when they saw the movie star, a few years older than in his films but still a great actor.

Use a comma to separate three or more words, phrases, or clauses that form a series.

> The professor was intelligent, articulate, and well prepared.

Use a comma to separate elements in addresses, geographical names, dates, and groups of three-digit whole numerals.

> They live at 8507 Fernald Avenue, Morton Grove, Illinois 60053, U.S.A.
> Monday, January 17, 1968, was my sister's birthdate.
> Cali, Colombia, is one of my favorite cities.
> 1,739
> 5,234,987,620

The Semicolon

Use a semicolon to separate two independent clauses not separated by a period or by a comma and a coordinating conjunction. The use of a semicolon demonstrates that the two independent clauses are closely related.

> The teacher could not come today; all faculty members had to attend the university-wide meeting.
> He did not study at all this semester; his grade report of three *D*'s and two *F*'s surprised no one.

The semicolon can also be used (in the place of a period) when the second independent clause begins with a conjunctive adverb (e.g., *however, furthermore, moreover, therefore*).

> He wanted to attend the concert; however, he was forced to stay at home.
> Good writing requires deliberation and reflection; therefore, one should never put off assignments until the last minute.

Use a semicolon in a series to separate items that contain commas.

> He packed his shirts, sweaters, and pants in one bag; his toiletries and books in another; and his stereo, television, and radio in separate boxes.

The Colon

Use a colon to introduce a list. Do not use a colon after a form of the verb *be*.

> We need to order the following equipment: two color video recorders, seventeen cases of VHS tape, and two color monitors.

Use a colon to introduce a formal quotation.

> Professor Jones closed the convention when he stated: "Now we need to return to our classrooms and put our new-found theories into practice."

Use a colon to introduce a word, phrase, or clause that amplifies, explains, or summarizes the preceding sentence.

> The source of political power is easily traced: money.
> Education is the answer to the problems of the world: without it, humanity will continue to suffer its current ills.

Use a colon to separate minutes from hours.

Classes start promptly at 8:35 a.m.

Parentheses

Use parentheses to indicate information that may be helpful but is not strictly necessary for the sentence.

Philosophy classes (particularly those at the introductory level) are recommended for all students.
The correct use of punctuation (as well as grammar and mechanics) demonstrates a student's control of written English.

The Dash

Use a pair of dashes to show an emphatic interruption in the normal flow of a sentence.

The problems of the freshman student—which should be our real concern—are due to many factors.

Use a dash to indicate emphasis or contrast.

All the politicians speak of peace—while they approve funds for missiles.

The dash is used to set off parenthetical elements to which the writer wishes to give greater emphasis than possible with commas or parentheses.

Quotation Marks

Use quotation marks when writing the title of short works (e.g., poems, songs, short stories, chapters, articles). Do not use quotation marks with the titles of your own essays.

I have always enjoyed the poem "This Is Just To Say" by William Carlos Williams.

Use quotation marks to indicate direct quotations.

Then the advisor told me, "Do what you think is best."

Use a set of single quotation marks to enclose a quotation inside a quotation.

Advice is often long remembered after it is given. As Samuels wrote, "I have always kept close to me my uncle's words: 'Never forget your purpose in your work.' "

Put periods and commas inside the end quotation marks; colons and semicolons are placed outside the end quotation marks. Put exclamation marks and question marks inside or outside the end quotation marks, depending upon whether the marks punctuate the quotation or the entire sentence.

> Then he asked, "When will it be finished?"
>   (Only the quotation is a question.)
> Why did you say, "I don't think I like that course"?
>   (The entire sentence is a question.)

The Apostrophe

Use an apostrophe plus the letter *s* to show possession. After a word that ends in the letter *s*, add only the apostrophe.

> The chauffeur drove the mayor's car to the airport.
> The girls' soccer team won the city championship.

Use an apostrophe plus the letter *s* to form plurals of letters, numbers, and words referred to as such.

> He still needed some practice with his *g*'s.
> The winning lottery number contained five 7's.
> You should not use so many *and's* in your writing.

Use an apostrophe to show missing letters in a contraction. (Try to avoid contractions in academic writing, however.)

> Helen won't tell where she went.
> When he's finished, I'll let you know.

Remember not to confuse *it's* and *its*. The former is the contraction of *it is;* the latter is the possessive form of *it.*

The Hyphen

Use a hyphen to indicate compound words used as a single unit.

> Dean Drake was voted the most well-dressed administrator on campus.
> My sister-in-law is majoring in chemistry.
> up-to-date

Use a hyphen to indicate the division of a word at the end of a line (use only between syllables). Be sure to check a dictionary if you are not sure where the syllable divisions are.

> Only a small fraction of today's educational process is seen by most people.

Use a hyphen with compound numbers from twenty-one through ninety-nine. Also use it with fractions to separate the numerator from the denominator.

> fifty-four
> three hundred ninety-seven
> one-half
> seven-eighths

The Underline

Use an underline to indicate titles of books, journals, newspapers, all publications issued separately, and names of ships, works of art, movies, television and radio programs, and record albums.

> My nephews saw <u>Return of the Jedi</u> seventeen times.
> The required text for the business class is called <u>Business Principles for the Twentieth Century</u>.

Use an underline to indicate words, letters, or numbers referred to as such.

> Keep in mind the difference between <u>effect</u> and <u>affect</u>.
> Children have problems writing their <u>b</u>'s and <u>d</u>'s.
> Many people write a <u>7</u> with a cross line through the verticle stroke.

Use an underline to indicate words or phrases not yet accepted into English.

> <u>Kebsah</u>, a dish of rice and meat, is very popular in Saudi Arabia.
> A three-wheeled taxi-scooter is called a <u>samlor</u> in Thailand.

MECHANICS

Along with punctuation, mechanics are also important in writing. Correct usage of capitalization and numbers, accurate spelling, legible handwriting, and proper manuscript form all demonstrate that the writer is competent in these areas and, more importantly, has recognized that the reader has certain expectations that must be respected.

Not only can mistakes in mechanics change the meaning of your words ("I live in the white house" and "I live in the White House" convey *very* different messages—only the President of the United States could make the second statement), but they can also make your writing impossible to understand (if spelling errors are numerous or the handwriting is difficult to decipher). When you do the final editing of your papers, remember the points of mechanics discussed in this section.

Capitalization

Capitalize the first word in a sentence.

> Winter is the best time of year for some people.

Capitalize proper nouns, i.e., the names of people, cities, countries, and so on. Only the first letter of each name should be a capital letter.

> William James
> Tokyo
> Yugoslavia

Capitalize the names of specific organizations, places, buildings, and so on.

> the Organization of Petroleum Exporting Countries
> Times Square
> the John Hancock Center

Capitalize the first word of a quotation if it is a complete sentence.

> The mayor then said, "Welcome to our city!"

Capitalize the days of the week, months, and holidays.

> It always seems that Monday is the worst day of the week.
> I like December more than any other month—Christmas comes at the end.

Capitalize the names of deities, religions, and other terms of sacred significance.

> The Moslems follow the laws of Allah, the Christians the commandments of God, and the Buddhists the teachings of Buddha.

Capitalize all words in a title except for articles, short prepositions, and conjunctions. The first word of a title is always capitalized.

He must have read *The Call of the Wild* fourteen times.
I think I will title my autobiography *Short but Sweet.*

Capitalize languages, races, nationalities, and their corresponding adjectives.

The student signed up for chemistry, English, accounting, and Modern Greek.
The Japanese are famous for their technological innovations.

DO NOT capitalize general terms unless the term is a title or part of a name.

a professor (but Professor Andrews)
a president (but President Clark)
a company (but the Dallas Finance Company)
an aunt (but Aunt Sally)
my father (but Father)

DO NOT capitalize areas of study unless it is the name of a specific class.

economics (but Economics 101)
art history (but Art History 324)

DO NOT capitalize the names of the seasons.

fall, winter, spring, summer

DO NOT capitalize the directions of the compass unless they refer to a specific geographical location.

The plane traveled southwest for four hours.
The Southwest is a warm part of the United States.

Numbers

Write out numbers that are two words or less. Numbers with three or more words should be expressed in figures (some fields use a different rule; check with your instructor).

The pilot has flown sixty-four missions.
The accident fatality count just reached 253.

Write out a number if it occurs at the beginning of a sentence, regardless of the number of words it uses.

Three hundred twenty-five trees were struck by lightning.

Be consistent with numbers in a series: either use figures for all of the numbers or write out all of the numbers (if one number should be in figures, use figures for all of them).

> They ordered ninety-three hammers, eighty-four saws, and seventy-five screwdrivers.
> The doctor saw 86 patients in May, 37 in June, and 102 in July.

The following numbers should be expressed in figures:

dates:	June 18, 1969
addresses:	1734 Springdale Drive
decimals:	.003
dimensions:	8½ × 11 in.
percentages:	54 percent
page numbers:	page 246
chapters:	Chapter 6
telephone numbers:	(703) 663-7894
money:	$6.98

Spelling

Although the English spelling system is difficult to master, accurate spelling is essential. Whenever you write, you should have a good monolingual English dictionary to check your spelling. You could also ask an American friend to go over your paper to identify words that are misspelled. If you know you have problems with spelling, keep a notebook to write out the words you have misspelled in your essays. Study it a few minutes each day (you could even tape a list of especially difficult words on your bathroom mirror, and study them while you brush your teeth—or over the kitchen sink, and learn while you wash dishes). These problem words in your notebook or on your list will probably be words you have actually used, and most likely you will use them again. Take time to memorize the spelling so that you can use them correctly in the future. The fewer spelling mistakes you have in your papers, the less distracted your reader will be.

Handwriting

Unless you type your papers, handwriting is another consideration in your writing. Your readers have to be able to read what you write. This is true for test questions or for essays. Your teachers, as well as all readers, will be distracted from your ideas if they have to decipher your writing word by word. Research shows that poor handwriting can distract from the content and organization of your papers; therefore, try to write as legibly as possible. This is especially true for students whose first language uses an alphabet different from the English one, but it is also true for American students and students whose native language uses a similar alphabet.

Manuscript Form

The following are suggestions to make your written homework more acceptable in appearance. Just as people are often judged by their appearances, so are papers. Neat, orderly papers make a good initial impression. Employees in the working world would never hand their bosses reports that do not look professional; neither should you give your teachers material that is not in an acceptable form.

- Use white paper. Blue, pink, or green paper may be attractive, but it makes reading your work more difficult for the teacher. If you are writing your paper by hand, use lined paper—not typing paper or graph paper.
- Write on one side of the paper only. If you write on both sides, the ink often shows through (think of a typed report—it is written on only one side).
- Observe the margins on both the left and right sides of the paper. Clear margins make your writing look nicer and easier to read. Using the right margin also prevents your running out of space at the end of the line. It is perfectly all right to go slightly over the right margin to finish writing a word—something you cannot do if you reach the edge of the paper.
- Use a good pen, with blue or black ink. Green, red, or brown ink is hard to read. Similarly, do not turn in a homework assignment written in pencil. Your final draft should always be in ink.
- Do your best to turn in a paper that looks clean and neat. Avoid excessive cross-outs or inserted words. If necessary, rewrite the paper. Or use a pen with erasable ink.

Keep in mind that you want the content of your papers to be as clear and accessible to the reader as possible. If the outward appearance of your papers does not distract your readers from the content, you start out with an advantage. The appearance of a paper alone does not guarantee a good product, but if combined with thoughtful, developed, and well-organized content, you will have mastered an important purpose of your English class and your academic study in general.

Transitions

EXEMPLIFICATION

1. Fruits are good diet foods. *For example,* / *To illustrate,* / *For instance,* a whole cantaloupe contains only 70 calories.

2. The brochure dealt with traveling in Morocco. *That is,* / *In other words,* / *Namely,* it discussed transportation, accommodations, food, climate, currency, and language.

3. Computer technology affects nearly all aspects of our lives. *An example of this* can be seen in the pricing codes imprinted on packages at the supermarkets.

4. We still needed to arrange several details for the trip. *Specifically,* we had to make plane and hotel reservations as well as decide on the final itinerary.

5. Our eyes do not always function as we believe they should. *Frequently,* they give us information that is not accurate.

6. I sometimes do not know when to leave my roommate alone. *A case in point* occurred this morning.

7. Shopping in small markets is usually quite advantageous. *In particular,* one can find specialty items that the larger stores do not carry.

117

ENUMERATION/SEQUENCE

1. Charge cards can be used to pay for dining, traveling, and shop-
   ping. *In addition,* some can be used to pay medical expenses.

   Moreover,
   In addition,
   Furthermore,
   Also,

2. *First* eat the avocado. *Afterwards,* plant the pit for a quickly
   growing indoor plant.

   Then,
   Afterwards,
   Next,

3. *Another* sense that we take for granted is the sense of touch.
4. Fold the paper in half. Then fold it in half *again*.

COMPARISON

1. Word processors *not only* help writers rearrange word order, *but*
   they *also* can check spelling.
2. Everyone knows that humans have five-digit hands. Skeletons of
   whales reveal that their fins are *similarly* five-digited.

   also
   similarly
   likewise

3. Just as man is omnivorous, so *too* is the bear.
4. Gliders soar through the sky *in the same* basic *manner* as the
   large condor.

   way
   manner

CONTRAST

1. Man soon will be able to travel through space. *However,* he will
   never be able to conquer it.

   Yet,
   However,
   But,

2. Although urban development destroys the ecological balance, it
   nevertheless provides needed employment for many people.

   still
   nevertheless
   nonetheless
   Though

3. *Even though* we have seen many successes in medical research,
   there is still much to learn.

   Even though
   Although

4. *Despite* the small size of an ant, it is tremendously strong.
5. John likes to wear T-shirts and bluejeans. *In contrast,* Paul always dresses as if he were going to a formal dinner.
6. Many people believe that work is the greatest virtue of all. But,
   on the contrary, it leads only to a tired life.

   in fact,
   on the contrary,

7. *Unlike* the small serrano pepper, the large bell pepper is sweet and not at all hot.

8. *In spite of* the dangers of being in an earthquake area, many people would live nowhere but in San Francisco.

9. West Texas is a flat, desolate land. *On the other hand,* East Texas has tall stands of green pine trees.

10. Dogs love taking orders from their masters. Cats, *conversely,* do not pay too much attention to the people around them.

11. The doctor told me to stay away from rich food, *yet* I cannot stop dreaming about cakes and pies at night.

12. My father always folds his napkin when he leaves the table *whereas* my mother crumples hers up in a ball.

RESULT

1. Sports fans today seem to expect athletes to be larger-than-life
   heroes.   *As a result,* / *Consequently,* / *Hence,*   spectators have lost sight of sports as
   healthy competition.

2. *Because* people in certain societies are afraid of growing old, they treat the elderly as a threat to their society.

3. The supervisor told the employees to arrive on time. *Accordingly,* everyone showed up at 8:00 sharp.

4. I needed a rest, *so* I went to the mountains for a week.

5. The modern day person faces many pressures.
   Thus, / *As a consequence,* / *Therefore,* / *For this reason,*   doctors are seeing many patients with
   severe psychological disturbances.

EMPHASIS

1. Businesses that reward their employees with substantial raises, bonuses, and benefits *indeed* / *Truly,* grow more successful than businesses that do not.

2. *As a matter of fact,* / *Surely,* when people can communicate with each other, they get along better.

3. Television addiction does not occur only among adults. *Even* / *Certainly* preschool children suffer from this habit.

4. *Undoubtedly* one of the greatest men of our time was Mahatma Gandhi.

5. *Again*, Gandhi was one of the greatest humanitarians the world has seen.

6. The nuclear bomb, *obviously*, casts the most fearful shadow of them all.

SUMMARY

In short,

1. *On the whole,*   effective coherence in writing depends upon
In conclusion,
smooth sentence-to-sentence transitions.
To sum up,

2. *To conclude,*   living in a solar-heated house can be beneficial
To summarize,
in several ways.

in brief,

3. The findings of the research to date,   *in summary,*   suggest that not all the answers have been found.

Revision

The following five pages show the stages of revision from the original through the reorganizing, deleting, and adding revisions to the final version.

ORIGINAL VERSION

Women were treated as creatures on earth with no rights and as housewives and as human beings only for raising children and for sexual pleasure of men. Years ago, moreover, women were shut up by their husbands. They could not share anything with their partners, either inside the house or outside. For example, to help each other to solve a problem concerning their life or their children, or to discuss a subject whatever it is about. Women must always say "yes" and agree with their husbands even though they have a different opinion. During the first centuries and throughout the earliest part of the nineteenth century, women were still excluded from all their rights. For example, right of voting, to work outside the house, and to be educated as well.

Man has treated his wife as a housewife, or as a kind of human being created to raise the children and do the housework. Moreover, she has to do all that in a limited area. Further, the allowable range of behavior is greater in the male than in the female, so that a male generally has more responsibility and freedom to act than a female. All that makes a woman feel unappreciated. It seems like she is a twenty-four hour worker with no holidays, and she can't be ill even if she is. She doesn't have enough power to express her feelings about her situation and her depression. Most of the time she is treated as a slave inside the house.

At the same time, man has treated his wife as a being to satisfy his sexual desires regardless of whether it's appropriate for her or not. Sometimes all that leads her toward a bad situation, one caused by man. For example, a woman commits suicide in order to get rid of that kind of life forever because she tried every all way to be treated at least as a human being. In conclusion, a woman is a human being with the same rights as a man. This is true in every field like education, jobs, leader of the country (as in England and India recently), and in different jobs. It must be known that she is not a creature that a man can use whenever he wants.

REORGANIZING REVISION

Women were treated as creatures on earth with no rights and as housewives and as human beings only for raising children and for sexual pleasure of men. Years ago, moreover, women were shut up by their husbands. They could not share anything with their partners, either inside the house or outside. For example, to help each other to solve a problem concerning their life or their children, or to discuss a subject whatever it is about. Women must always say "yes" and agree with their husbands even though they have a different opinion. During the first centuries and throughout the earliest part of the nineteenth century, women were still excluded from all their rights. For example, right of voting, to work outside the house, and to be educated as well.

[margin note: What type of introduction: general → specific past → present]

[margin note: Needs clear thesis — what is the main point?]

[margin note: Topic Sentence has two ideas →]

Man has treated his wife as a housewife, or as a kind of human being created to raise the children and do the housework. Moreover, she has to do all that in a limited area. Further, the allowable range of behavior is greater in the male than in the female, so that a male generally has more responsibility and freedom to act than a female. All that makes a woman feel unappreciated. It seems like she is a twenty-four hour worker with no holidays, and she can't be ill even if she is. She doesn't have enough power to express her feelings about her situation and her depression. Most of the time she is treated as a slave inside the house.

[margin note: Same time as what? Expand transition]

At the same time, man has treated his wife as a being to satisfy his sexual desires regardless of whether it's appropriate for her or not. Sometimes all that leads her toward a bad situation, one caused by man. For example, a woman commits suicide in order to get rid of that kind of life forever because she tried every all way to be

treated at least as a human being. (¶) In conclusion, a woman is a human being with the same rights as a man. This is true in every field like education, jobs, leader of the country (as in England and India recently), and in different jobs. It must be known that she is not a creature that a man can use whenever he wants.

[margin note: Make into separate paragraph]

[margin note: What type of closing is this? Call to action? Summary?]

DELETING REVISION

Women were treated as creatures on earth with no rights and as housewives and as human beings only for raising children and for sexual pleasure of men. Years ago, moreover, women were shut up by their husbands. They could not share anything with their partners, either inside the house or outside. ~~For example, to help each other to solve a problem concerning their life of their children, or to discuss a subject whatever it is about.~~ Women must always say "yes" and agree with their husbands even though they have a different opinion. During the first centuries and throughout the earliest part of the nineteenth century, women were still excluded from all their rights. ~~For example, right of voting, to work outside the house, and to be educated as well.~~

What type of introduction: general→specific past→present

]need? delete?   sentence goes off topic

Needs clear thesis — What is the main point?

Topic Sentence has two ideas →

Man has treated his wife as a housewife, or as a kind of human being created to raise the children and do the housework. Moreover, she has to do all that in a limited area. ~~Further, the allowable range of behavior is greater in the male than in the female, so that a male generally has more responsibility and freedom to act than a female. All that makes a woman feel unappreciated.~~ It seems like she is a twenty-four hour worker with no holidays, and she can't be ill even if she is. ~~She doesn't have enough power to express her feelings about her situation and her depression.~~ Most of the time she is treated as a slave inside the house.

]delete? what does "limited area" mean?

Same time as what? Expand transition

At the same time, man has treated his wife as a being to satisfy his sexual desires regardless of whether it's appropriate for her or not. Sometimes all that leads her toward a bad situation, one caused by man. For example, a woman commits suicide in order to get rid of that kind of life forever because she tried every all way to be ~~treated at least as a human being.~~ ⑨ In conclusion, a woman is a human being with the same rights as a man. This is true in every field like education, jobs, leader of the country (as in England and India recently), and in different jobs. It must be known that she is not a creature that a man can use whenever he wants.

]this does not illustrate or support the topic sentence delete

Make into separate paragraph

conclusion does not follow body— introduces a new idea

What type of closing is this? Call to action? Summary?

ADDING REVISION

⟵ — *Title*

What type of introduction: general → specific past → present

Women were treated as creatures on earth with no rights and as housewives and as human beings only for raising children and for sexual pleasure of men. Years ago, moreover, women were shut up by their husbands. They could not share anything with their partners, either inside the house or outside. ~~For example, to help each other to solve a problem concerning their life or their children, or to discuss a subject whatever it is about.~~ Women must always say "yes" and agree with their husbands even though they have a different opinion. During the first centuries and throughout the earliest part of the nineteenth century, women were still excluded from all their rights. ~~For example, right of voting, to work outside the house, and to be educated as well.~~

need? delete? *sentence goes off topic*

Add thesis

Needs clear thesis — what is the main point?

Topic Sentence has two ideas →

Man has treated his wife as a housewife, or as a kind of human being created to raise the children and do the housework. Moreover, she has to do all that in a limited area. ~~Further, the allowable range of behavior is greater in the male than in the female, so that a male generally has more responsibility and freedom to act than a female. All that makes a woman feel unappreciated.~~ It seems like she is a twenty-four hour worker with no holidays, and she can't be ill even if she is. ~~She doesn't have enough power to express her feelings about her situation and her depression.~~ Most of the time she is treated as a slave inside the house.

delete? What does "limited area" mean?

Add details

Add examples/ illustrations

Same time as what? Expand transition

Need subpoints and illustrations

At the same time, man has treated his wife as a being to satisfy his sexual desires regardless of whether it's appropriate for her or not. Sometimes all that leads her toward a bad situation, one caused by man. For example, a woman commits suicide in order to get rid of that kind of life forever because she tried every all way to be ~~treated at least as a human being.~~ (¶) In conclusion,

this does not illustrate or support the topic sentence — delete

Make into separate paragraph

Conclusion does not follow body — introduces a new idea

a woman is a human being with the same rights as a man. This is true in every field like education, jobs, leader of the country (as in England and India recently), and in different jobs. It must be known that she is not a creature that a man can use whenever he wants.

What type of closing is this? Call to action? Summary?

Add/rework conclusion

FINAL VERSION

Unequal Partners

During the first centuries and throughout the earliest parts of the nineteenth century, women had been excluded from many of their rights as human beings. Women were shut up by their husbands; they could not share anything with their partners, either inside the house or outside. Throughout much of the world today, the same situation still holds true. The position of married women in their own households still needs much improvement.

Men have treated their wives as beings created only to work. The wife is a twenty-four hour worker with no holidays. When the rest of the community is home from work for a holiday, she must keep active, cleaning, cooking, and taking care of the children. Even if she is ill, she cannot take time off. Most of the time she is treated as a slave inside the house. She has to follow her master's orders. While her husband relaxes in front of the television, she still has to plan the next day's meals and organize the family's activities. Unlike the husband, the housewife never has any free time.

At the same time that the man uses his wife as a working machine, he also treats her as a being to gratify his sexual desires. No matter what time of day, she is expected to satisfy him. When the husband comes home at night, she has to be alluring and attractive whether she likes it or not. If he wants romance with her, she has to agree and fulfill his fantasies. When they wake up in the morning, she has to be attentive to his needs and make him feel like a man. Most husband-wife relationships have been one-sided.

In conclusion, wives have often been treated as inferior creatures with no rights of their own. It is time to realize that women are not creatures that men can use as they want. If women can be leaders of nations, such as in England and India, surely women can be equal partners in their own homes.

Professional Essays

The Advantages of Running

JAMES F. FIXX

Even if we grant that there are other sports that are as good for one's health as running, there remain good reasons to choose running. One is the time devoted to it. When I played tennis, I was a member of a regular foursome who played from nine to eleven every Saturday and Sunday. What with time for dressing, showering and driving to and from the courts, I was spending six hours a weekend at tennis. Furthermore, I was burning up 2,000 calories at most. Nowadays, unless I am trying to put in high mileage to get ready for a marathon, I run ten miles a day—a total, on a weekend, of almost two and a half hours, and even the world's longest showers could not possibly raise it to more than three hours. Thus in half the time it used to require, I get the same 2,000 calories' worth of exercise.

1.

An incidental benefit is that running widows or widowers, if not unknown, are at least rare. Even a long run can be tucked away in some unnoticed corner of the day—either early in the morning or at a time when other members of the family are busy with cooking, homework or other activities. All it takes is some foresight and good manners.

2.

The inner spirit of running is also different from that of most other sports. It can be as competitive or noncompetitive as you choose to make it. In touch football, there's no convenient way not to try hard. In tennis, you've got to try to put the ball out of your opponent's reach. Golfers become so immersed in the game that they tie themselves into tense, tangled knots even during a friendly round. Runners, on the other hand, can run as gently or as hard as they want to.

3.

With a stopwatch you can try to run a course faster than you've ever done it before. You can attempt to run your friends into the ground, or you can treat a run as if it were nothing more than a romp through the countryside, bouncing along only hard enough to set the juices to bubbling gently. Even in a race there's no need to run at full throttle if you don't want to. You'll get a good work-out even if you run at less-than-maximum speed.

4.   Many runners, some of them very good ones, never race at all. All they want is fitness and the good feelings that come from a daily run. Jack Gianino is one such runner. He puts in an hour and a half a day in Central Park and even when acting assignments take him out of town never misses a day. But Gianino does not race. "I tried it and I didn't like all that hard breathing," he says.

5.   The noncompetitiveness of running makes it a perfect family sport. If a man wants to run ten miles, he can run the first two miles with his wife and children, then drop the kids off and run a second loop with his wife alone. When she's had her four-mile run, he can go bashing off through the countryside for a few more miles.

6.   Running is also probably the world's most democratic sport. Runners are almost totally lacking in discrimination based on race, sex, age, class or any-thing else. At a recent race in New York City I saw a cardiologist, an orthopedic surgeon, and a preventive medicine specialist for a major corporation, a foundry worker and a printer, a retired postman and a shoe salesman, a judge, an au-thor, and a filmmaker, a Rockefeller Foundation executive and a man who has long been on unemployment, along with an assortment of office workers, housewives, students and senior citizens. If they met at a cocktail party instead of a race I suspect they would not have much in common, but here there was little if any sense of social hierarchy. Running is an egalitarian and distinctly unsnobbish sport, one that meshes with much that is excellent in the American spirit.

7.   I would be misleading you if I tried to force upon you the impression that there is nothing wrong with running. You can be forced into a ditch by a car. You can get Achilles tendinitis or a pulled muscle. You can find yourself, at five o'clock on a January morning, cursing the moment you first thought of run-ning. (Don't worry; you'll feel fine once you get moving.)

Discussion Questions: Essay 1

(Persuasion—*Fixx*)

1. List some of the characteristics the intended audience for this es-say probably possesses.
2. Where is the thesis statement?
3. Even though the first sentence and the last paragraph suggest possible opposition, the structure of the essay as a whole does not deal with opposing arguments. How many reasons does Fixx give for running? What are they?
4. Identify the topic sentences introducing each of the reasons. Where in each paragraph are they found?
5. In Paragraph 1, notice that Fixx supports his point by giving

specific data on hours, calories, and miles. What other tactic does he use in this paragraph to emphasize an advantage of running?

6. Paragraphs 3 and 4 are actually one unit—they both develop the same point. What kind of evidence does Fixx provide in paragraph 4? Do you think it is effective?

7. In paragraph 6, Fixx identifies sixteen runners. Why did Fixx go to this trouble?

8. Does Fixx use transitions to link his paragraphs together? What are they?

9. In 1984, James Fixx died of a heart attack while running. Does this affect the persuasiveness of his essay?

ESSAY 2: PERSUASION

The Hunting Ethic

HERBERT E. DOIG

Few resources stir the emotional stability of the people of this world more than wildlife. It is logical then for points of view to conflict, when values associated with wildlife differ. Such is the case with hunting as a use of wildlife and the philosophy of preservation which to some offers the only hope for perpetuation of the resource.   1.

In an obvious attempt to avoid being placed in the center of this conflict, I will approach the sensitive subject of hunting objectively, recognizing its values and its shortcomings through the eyes of a professional biologist responsible for a program with primary concern for the perpetuation of wildlife as a part of the total ecology of the state. It is important to add that in this context conservation is viewed as the wise use of natural resources for the good of mankind and that man is an element of his environment and not the master of it.   2.

It is necessary to understand some basic truths if one is to assess objectively the ethics of hunting and its effect on wildlife populations. Wildlife represent a renewable resource that cannot be stockpiled for the enjoyment of future generations. All species produce an annual surplus that will be removed by predation, disease, parasites and, if allowed to exceed available food supplies, starvation. Many species undergo annual mortality rates that may exceed 70 percent and are perpetuated by a compensating reproductive rate.   3.

As wildlife abundance increases some species become a nuisance to man, compete with him for food or destroy the products of his labor. Wildlife are flexible and react to changes in the environment, frequently becoming more abundant as habitats more nearly satisfy basic survival needs.   4.

Since his origin on earth man has functioned as a predator on the wildlife with which he has come into contact. This role has been strengthened with the development of weapons while his dependence upon prey for survival has diminished with time. The pressures man applies to wildlife populations are not significantly different from those of other predators except in degree and the beneficial aspects of the predator-prey relationship also exist. The removal of the weaker individuals in a population usually results in a strengthening of the   5.

species, thus enabling its perpetuation under changing environmental conditions. Man is an efficient predator and in some instances represents the only harvester of a growing population.

6.   Man's reliance upon wildlife for meat has greatly diminished in this country but enjoyment of the savory flavor of a game dinner still remains. The value of the meat alone, however, does not sustain the popularity of hunting. It is the physical, emotional and often spiritual rewards that are associated with a day out-of-doors that attract many and establish hunting as a traditional recreational endeavor. Unless personally involved, few can appreciate the identity of man with the land that occurs when a person enjoys a quiet place to hunt and the natural habitat where game can thrive.

7.   The benefits from hunting are not enjoyed by the hunter alone. Sportsmen through the purchase of licenses and permits willingly finance programs designed to protect and enhance wildlife resources. In 1925 the sportsmen of New York sponsored a law that led to the establishment of the Conservation Fund which for many years represented the only source of revenue for wildlife management and research programs in the state. This fund has been used to effectively enforce laws and regulations designed to protect all wildlife. Moneys have also supported a wide spectrum of programs that have ultimately led to the preservation and improvement of habitats essential to the continued welfare of the resources.

8.   In 1937 Congress established the Pittman-Robertson Act, which provided for moneys derived from an 11 percent tax on arms and ammunition to be returned to the states on a cost share basis and to be used for wildlife habitat restoration and research. Until recently when general tax revenues have supplemented these sources of funds, it was the sportsman who alone paid the bills for wildlife conservation in the state.

9.   Hunters through a strong organization have long supported conservation action on many fronts. In spite of their intense and often narrow interests, they stood firmly behind environmental cleanup efforts and were an influential force in the promotion of a healthy environment long before it was fashionable to do so. They have effectively used the legislative process to protect rather than exploit their interest in wildlife and have, as a group, exhibited a desire to do what is best even though some efforts have been misguided through a lack of knowledge.

10.   The nature of the hunter's interest and his investment of money through purchase of license fees have led to a somewhat narrow outlook which in some cases visualizes wildlife resource programs as serving game species at the exclusion of other wildlife. This bias is gradually changing and most hunters are recognizing the values of all wildlife and are supporting programs that will benefit all species. It is not difficult to understand the restrictive nature of the hunter's interest when wildlife programs have been and continue to be funded with moneys derived from the sale of hunting licenses.

11.   The recent manifestation of social awareness of environmental problems has stimulated the development of an attitude that supports preservation as the only hope for the future of wildlife. Those expressing this point of view believe that hunting destroys and that overexploitation will lead to the extinction of the hunted species. Quite to the contrary, properly regulated hunting cannot lead to the extinction or even the endangering of any species. Witness the fact that

none of the hunted species under modern fish and game management pro-grams has ever become extinct or endangered. Enlightened wildlife manage-ment currently guided by competent staffs of professional wildlife biologists at the state and federal level, will lead to the strengthening of protective measures for rare and endangered species and for those species that are most vulnerable to environmental pressures. At the same time programs that permit regulated harvest and utilization of the annual surplus of game can be continued without significant adverse effect on any species.

A second major motivating force supporting the preservationist philoso-phy concerns the humane treatment of animals. It is suggested that the killing of wildlife with firearms is inhumane and that hunting should be stopped to per-mit the peaceful pursuit of life by all living things. Supporters of this position should familiarize themselves with the true characteristics of the environment around them. It is soon evident to the student of nature that life in our environ-ment is violent and that few individuals of any wild species survive to enjoy the amenities of old age. The natural forces of predation and starvation are savage and often result in a lingering death. Man through hunting is performing his traditional role as a predator in the environment and utilizes the prey to his best advantage. The application of his technique of harvest is seldom less humane than the inevitable death of the animal through what often is referred to as natu-ral causes.

A third argument used by the opponents of hunting is impossible to ra-tionalize. A segment of the human society views killing as a moral issue and feels that there is no justification in our sophisticated culture for causing the death of another living thing. Like religion and politics, this view is seldom dis-cussed objectively.

In final analysis, the ethics of hunting gives rise to strong emotional conflicts. These conflicts are often polarized in uncompromising positions at opposite ends of the spectrum of reason. It is hoped that our society will accept the philosophy that there is room for both attitudes provided one does not try to force its views and beliefs on the other. Even more important, thinking men should not get lost in the fog of conflict but should look to solving the true prob-lems that threaten the future of wildlife populations; the ever-increasing danger of pollution; destruction of habitat by man's use of the land; incompatibility of wildlife with man's activities; forces of ecological change; and physical destruc-tion from highways, efficient farming and urban expansion.

The accomplishment of future goals shared by all regardless of their posi-tion on the issue of hunting requires a total commitment from all people to look realistically at wildlife and its renewable characteristics and to practice good stewardship and wise use which will assure the enjoyment of this valuable re-source by future generations.

Discussion Questions: Essay 2

(Persuasion—*Doig*)

1. Hunting is a controversial issue, which Doig acknowledges in the early part of his essay. What are the two different groups of people concerned about in this issue?

2. Paragraphs 1 and 2 open the essay; they make the reader aware of the problem. Although Doig does not offer his personal view in a thesis statement, he does state the purpose of his essay. Where is this found?

3. Although Doig says he is looking at his subject objectively, it is obvious that he does take a side. Which side is he on?

4. What is the purpose of paragraphs 3 and 4?

5. Doig is using a variation of an essay addressing an opposing audience. Notice, however, that his refutation section is put last. Paragraphs 5 through 10 present points supporting hunting. What are these points? (Do not use paragraphs as an indicator. Sometimes two points may be found in one paragraph, or one point may be discussed in two paragaphs.)

6. The first sentence of paragraph 7 is a transition; the second is the topic sentence. In paragraphs 7 and 8, how does Doig support the point he is making in the topic sentence?

7. Paragraphs 11 through 13 present opposing arguments to hunting and Doig's refutations of these arguments. How does paragraph 13 differ from paragraphs 11 and 12? Do you think Doig's strategy in paragraph 13 was wise?

8. Doig closes his essay with paragraphs 14 and 15. What type of closing is this?

ESSAY 3: PERSUASION

The "Meaningless Mean": A Proposal to Simplify Academic Averages and Grades

JAMES A. HUSTON

1. Each year the No. 1 student in the freshman, sophomore, and junior classes at my college is awarded a class honor scholarship. Let us suppose that Student A has a 4.0 average—straight A's in 15 hours of work including English, chemistry, history, music, and French. Student B has exactly the same record—the same grades in the same subjects—but in addition has taken a one-hour laboratory in organic chemistry in which he received a B. Which student has the better record and should win the scholarship? To my mind, there is no question but that B has the better record. But the conventional rule says the award should go to the student with the highest grade-point average, so A who avoided the lab, would be the winner.

2. Some years ago we had a student who left at the end of his freshman year to go to Vietnam. He had received virtually all F's both semesters. Three years later, he returned and was readmitted for another try. He approached his academic work with a new enthusiasm, and in his first semester made a 3.5 average. But to be in good academic standing a student has to have a cumulative average of at least 1.5. His 3.5 was enough to make the dean's list, but when combined with two semesters of 0.1, it was not enough to keep him off probation. When he failed to get off probation the second semester—with another

performance worthy of the dean's list—he was subject to academic suspension for having an average below the required 1.5 for two semesters. Only a special waiver allowed him to continue, which he did in an outstanding way.

3.
Recently we had an honor graduate who missed *magna cum laude* by one-hundredth of a point because as a summer scholarship student at the college between his junior and senior years in high school he had received a B in a one-hour history course. It did not matter that he had earned A's in physics, Greek, art, philosophy, and religious studies—more quality points than some who came away with *magna* honors; he had had a B in a one-hour course as a high-school junior and now he had to be satisfied with *cum laude.*

4.
Students go to great lengths to avoid "hurting" their averages. Some will withdraw from a course if they do poorly on the first examination; others will attempt a "death-bed withdrawal" at the end of the semester when it appears that they are likely to fail. The whole pass-fail system has emerged to encourage students to try courses outside their major areas without being fearful of hurting their averages.

5.
A bad semester or a bad year, as in the case of the student who went to Vietnam, can have an albatross effect. Later it is not enough if he does as well as anyone else; he must do better. Someone who can do good work is required to do superior work to bring up his average. Simply because he failed in a couple of courses outside his major some time ago, why must a student have to do better than his fellow students just so he can bring up his cumulative average sufficiently to graduate?

6.
The whole academic world seems to be enamored of index numbers and averages—the "meaningless mean." Instructors often speak of having to average their grades. Why? Why is it not enough simply to add up the total points in the grade book for each student? Grade-point averages have about as much meaning as annual temperature: Little Rock has about the same mean annual temperature as Honolulu, but what does that signify, when the extremes go from 118 to 17 at one and only from 93 to 53 at the other?

7.
What we need is a return to the simpler total-point system that a number of colleges employed a generation ago. A four-point scale could still be used, but it would be even simpler to go back to the three-point scale—that is, A = 3, B = 2, C = 1, D = 0 (with hours of credit), F = 0 (with no credit). Thus the normal requirement might be 124 credit hours *and* 124 quality points. A student who took and passed just 124 hours would have a C average, but the average would not govern. If a student had failed a course, or had too many D's, he could make up the deficiency by taking additional courses (repeating a course if it were required, or taking something else if not) and earning the necessary quality points. He would not have to earn above-average grades to bring up his average.

8.
No longer would it be necessary to have elaborate rules for repeating courses to "remove" F's. No longer would it be necessary to have a pass-fail system so that students won't have to worry about hurting their averages when they dare to take a difficult or unusual course. No longer would it be necessary to make exceptions for a student to resume work simply because he has had a bad semester, perhaps in a different field. No longer would a student be penalized in academic standing or scholarship competition for doing work beyond the minimum requirement.

9.   Honors could be calculated in the same way as graduation requirements. For example, the dean's list might include all students who earned at least 40 points in a semester, or it might include those in the upper 10 per cent in points for the semester. Similarly, any student might be graduated *magna cum laude* if he earned a total of as many as 335 quality points, or if he were in, say, the upper 5 per cent of graduates in terms of quality points earned. Under that system, Student *B* in the example given above would have been rewarded for taking the organic-chemistry laboratory instead of being penalized, and would have won the scholarship.

10.   "But," someone will say, "suppose that student had taken a course in bait casting or basket weaving just to pad his score?" My answer would be, More power to him; he did it in addition to the other things. Still, I would limit to 18 the number of hours that a student could take in a semester.

11.   Now what about the grades themselves? We have no agreed-upon philosophy of grades or of normal distribution. We have no consistent way of determining grades. What we have is a pool of subjective judgments carried to the second decimal place in carefully calculated averages used to determine success or failure, honors or academic probation, admission to graduate and professional schools, and justification for years of work and expense. Surely with all the emphasis on grades and precise averages, a student has the right to expect a certain level of consistency among professors and academic departments in the assignment of grades.

12.   What should a grade represent? Performance in relation to some absolute standard that the professor has in mind? Performance in relation to fellow students—that is, "on the curve"? Performance in terms of the student's own improvement during the semester? Should it be a reward for conscientious effort, to encourage students to try harder? A reward for being a nice fellow, or a punishment for being tardy or uncooperative?

13.   My own feeling is that a grade ought to represent a degree of mastery of a subject in terms of what students—now and in the past—have been able to do in a particular course. I like to take the top score for each graded activity—quiz, examination, paper, recitation—and add them up. Allowance can be made for an unusual genius by looking at the second-highest scores, and for a mediocre class by looking at scores from previous years. Still, by relying on scores that some student or students actually made, one corrects in a way for inaccurate or unfair examinations, for example, and avoids basing grades on an unrealistic or arbitrary standard.

14.   Taking the sum of all the highest scores, I then apply the "harness-horse-racing rule." It used to be that any horse that had not reached a post one-sixteenth of a mile from the finish wire when the winner passed was declared to have been "distanced" and was ineligible to return for the next heat. On that basis, the students in the 70's, for example, get C; in the 80's, a B; and in the 90's, A. The actual percentages should be a matter of agreed-upon institutional policy, but it should be made clear.

15.   That system has the virtue of the curve in judging the performance of a student in relation to that of other students. It has the virtue of absolute scale in allowing any number to pass, or to get a certain grade, regardless of how many others scored the same.

16.   What is meant by "high academic standards"? Some professors seem to

think that they are synonymous with "tough" grading and long, laborious assignments. On the contrary, to me, high standards mean high expectations of mastery of a subject. An inordinately high failure rate can be as much a reflection on the professor as on the students. On the other hand, an inordinately high number of A's among students who have not really mastered what ought to be expected of them in a certain course at a certain level would be indicative of low academic standards. One ought to aim at as high a mastery of reasonably substantial material at a given level as possible.

17.

The horse-racing system of grading permits that mastery to be recognized. The total-point system of reckoning quality permits it to be rewarded on a far fairer and simpler basis than generally is possible under the system of the meaningless mean.

Discussion Questions: Essay 3

(Persuasion—*Huston*)

1. The audience of this essay is administrators and teachers at universities. Why did Huston choose to address these people as the audience (why are students not the intended audience)?
2. Paragraphs 1 through 6 constitute the introduction of this essay. Huston uses three specific examples from his own personal experience (paragraphs 1 through 3) and discusses the significance of these examples (paragraphs 4 through 6). Why do you think the author felt he needed to spend so much space developing the problem?
3. In paragraph 7, Huston presents his thesis. What is the rest of the paragraph devoted to?
4. Paragraph 8 is rather forceful. How did the author create this force?
5. What are the purposes of paragraphs 9 and 10?
6. In paragraphs 11 through 16, Huston introduces three questions. Why does he do this?
7. Most educational institutions would naturally be reluctant to change their grading policies. Do you think Huston has made a strong enough argument for his proposal? What would be some more opposing arguments?
8. What type of closing does Huston use to complete his essay?

ESSAY 4: EXEMPLIFICATION

A Matter of Interpretation

JAMES C. SIMMONS

So you are off to Japan but you don't know the language. That's all right, you tell yourself confidently. You'll get by on hand signals and body language. Everyone will understand those.

1.

2.   You'd better talk to Nancy Shepard about that. The high-school English teacher signed up for an exchange program through which she spent six weeks with a Japanese family on the outskirts of Tokyo. She spoke no Japanese and her family only limited English.

3.   "I thought I could always rely on hand gestures and signs when the going got rough," Shepard recalled later. "But I quickly learned they never worked as well as I had hoped. None of my hosts knew my sign language. One time when I pointed to my chest with my forefinger to indicate 'me,' I was shown to the bathroom because to the Japanese that same gesture means 'I want a bath.' The Japanese point their forefingers to their noses to mean 'me.' Then on another occasion I cracked my family up when I rubbed my thumb against my fingertips to give the American sign for money. To them that gesture meant I wanted to pick my nose! I had some embarrassing moments and a lot less communication than I had counted on back in California when I was planning my trip."

4.   Shepard had been initiated into a field largely ignored by most international travelers: body language. "Social intercourse depends heavily on the actions, postures, movements, and expressions of the talking bodies," writes Desmond Morris in his landmark study *Gestures.* "Words are good for facts and for ideas, but without gestures, human social life would become a cold and mechanical process."

5.   The fact is that all societies rely heavily on body language for basic communication. Yet few of these gestures carry universal meaning in today's world. One should no more expect the standard gestures of American society to be understood abroad than one would our slang. Sensitive travelers might do well to learn in advance something of the popular gestures of the countries they plan to visit and to learn which American gestures are common to other cultures and which are unique. Otherwise, the potential for embarrassing incidents is high. Consider the following:

6.   In Brazil people often add emphasis to a statement by snapping their fingers once with a whiplike motion of their hands. Brushing the tips of their fingers forward under their chins indicates, "I don't know."

7.   In Germany if a finger is pointed to one's head it means the other person is crazy. The unwary traveler who does this to a stranger can be arrested and fined, according to one obscure German law still on the books.

8.   Indians in Delhi grasp their ears to indicate repentance or sincerity. And Fijians fold their arms as a sign of respect when talking to someone. In Japan women will stick out their tongues to indicate embarrassment. And in much of the Middle East, raised eyebrows often mean "yes."

9.   The sophisticated traveler is sensitive to the subtle qualities of behavior—the use of gestures, the tone of voices, the dictates of space relationships (how closely does one stand when talking to someone)—that may build up feelings of frustration and hostility in people from a different culture. A little homework spent in advance on learning something of another people's gestures, customs, and language will repay rich dividends when one travels abroad.

10.   Where does the traveler go to get instruction? An excellent place to start is Morris's fascinating book, *Gestures,* the first serious attempt to map the geographical distribution of human gestures. Morris and his assistants studied the meanings and distributions of 20 of the most familiar European gestures,

including the fingertips kiss, the nose thumb, the forearm jerk, and the teeth flick. The results often were surprising.

11.
What can this mean for the typical traveler? Well, depending upon the circumstances, it may mean a great deal. In 1972, for example, three young American college men were sexually assaulted while hitchhiking across Turkey from Istambul to Ankara. As it turned out, their ignorance of Turkish hand gestures was their own worst enemy. In many parts of that country, extending the thumb upwards from the fist—the traditional American hand gesture requesting a ride from a passing motorist—conveys an altogether different meaning: an invitation for a homosexual encounter.

12.
In fact, when Morris and his colleagues researched the thumbs-up gesture, they learned that only 30 of their 1,200 informants at 40 locales in 25 countries identified it as indicating a hitch-hiker. The most widely held meaning for the gesture was "OK." In Sardinia and Greece the gesture transmitted the idea of "get stuffed," not a likely encouragement for passing drivers—unless they want to stop and pick a fight.

13.
Greeting friends is one of the world's most universal rituals. But the gestures associated with it vary widely from culture to culture. When strangers meet for the first time in the United States, a simple handshake is in order. However, in France the traditional American handshake is considered much too rough and rude; a quick handshake with only slight pressure is preferred. But throughout Latin America the greeting is often much more exuberant. A hearty embrace (abrazo) is common among men and women alike. The men often follow it with a friendly slap on the back. But in Ecuador, to greet a person without shaking hands is a sign of special respect.

14.
In the Far East the greeting ceremony is more complex. In India the handshake is not used except among westernized citizens; the preferred greeting is the namaste, in which the palms of the hand are placed together and the head is nodded. Throughout India it is quite rude to touch women, so never offer to shake their hands.

15.
The Japanese place great emphasis on formal courtesies and signs of respect. The bow, rather than the handshake, is the traditional form of greeting. The Japanese usually bow several times to each other upon meeting.

16.
Not even the gesture for waving good-by is standardized from one culture to another. In countries as far removed as Italy, Colombia, and China, people wave good-by with the palm and fingers moving back and forth, a beckoning signal to Americans. On the other hand, travelers in Malaysia should never beckon someone to come closer by moving their forefingers back and forth; the gesture is taken as an insult.

17.
In Spain the eyes provide important nonverbal clues. Spaniards who snap their eyelids are either angry or impatient. Spanish men also use eye contact to make "passes" on the street. If an unchaperoned woman avoids gazing boldly around as she walks down a street, then she will not be disturbed. However, should a man find a woman returning his stare, he may promptly attempt to start conversation.

18.
Even seemingly obvious gestures can be misunderstood. In parts of Europe, raising the index finger to signify "one"—be it for a Metro ticket, a postage stamp, or a souvenir—might net the unsuspecting traveler twice the

19.

amount anticipated. In much of Europe, when counting on one's fingers, "one" is often indicated by the thumb, "two" by the thumb and forefinger.

The language of gesture is so rife with pratfall potential that not even heads of state are immune. Desmond Morris points out that when British Prime Minister Margaret Thatcher made a V-for-victory sign for the television cameras in acknowledging an early election gain, she inadvertently showed the back of her hand rather than the palm—and thus presented the British viewing public with a gesture signifying no fewer than nine different obscenities.

Discussion Questions: Essay 4

(Exemplification—*Simmons*)

1. Identify the probable characteristics of the audience that the author is addressing.
2. What type of opening does Simmons use in paragraphs 1 through 3?
3. Which sentence in paragraphs 4 and 5 is the best candidate for the thesis statement?
4. Simmons' essay is full of examples. It opens with an example and gives six more examples in the introduction (if one considers the first nine paragraphs as introductory). How many other categories of examples does he use?
5. Why does Simmons use so many illustrations from different countries in each of his examples?
6. Simmons even uses an example for his closing. Examples are used to support a point. Were you convinced of the author's thesis?

ESSAY 5: COMPARISON OR CONTRAST ─────────────

Nursing Practices—England and America

MARY MADDEN

1.

I left my native Ireland after I had completed a high school education. I studied to become a nurse and midwife in England, and I eventually came to the United States of America. Because I have worked five years in hospitals in England and the U.S.A., my friends frequently ask about differences, as I see them, in the practice of nursing on both sides of the Atlantic.

2.

Until I realized how different the licensing laws of Great Britain are from those in the United States, I was surprised at the number of restrictions placed on a nurse's actions in this country. A nurse licensed in Britain may practice anywhere in the British Isles and in some countries abroad; in the United States, the nurse must apply in every state in which she hopes to work.

3.

In Britain, a nurse is a deeply respected, devoted woman, entrusted with a vast amount of responsibility. The patients place unquestioned confidence in her judgment and advice. The doctor relies on her report of her observations, and he seldom interferes in what is considered a nursing duty.

The nurse decides when the patient is allowed out of bed or what type of bath he may have. I do not recall ever seeing an order on a physician's chart such as "OOR in 24 hours" or "may take a shower." The nurse judges when a wound is healed and when sutures may be removed. She is always consulted about the patient's requirements and his progress. And because of the structure of most hospitals in England, the nurse is in view of the patient constantly. Whenever he needs attention, the nurse is there in the ward, and she may observe him, too, unobtrusively.   4.

Furthermore, the nurse is a member of the health team who sees the patient most frequently. To the patient she is the most familiar person in the strange hospital world.   5.

In the United States, the patient is likely to be under the care of the same doctor in and out of the hospital, so the doctor is the person the patient knows best and the one in whom he confides most easily. But though the patient's treatment and care are discussed with the nursing staff, a nurse is not allowed much freedom to advise a patient. Also, I have seen doctors visit patients without a word of communication to the nurse. Personally I think it difficult to be ignored when a patient's care is concerned and I think it prevents full utilization of the nurse's knowledge and skills.   6.

I myself found nursing practice easier, in a way, under the so-called "socialized medicine" of Great Britain than the more individual type of medical care found in the United States. It involved much less writing and left me at the patient's bedside where I am happiest. There was no need to write several charges and requests for the needs of the patient. Stocks of drugs and other medicines were kept on each ward, so that when medication was ordered, it was at hand. All charges were met by "National Health"—including all supplies and equipment used on the ward. The nurse tends a person who is free from much anxiety and hence more easily cared for while he is an inpatient.   7.

On the other hand, I found that my introduction to an American hospital was a happy experience. As a new nurse, I was guided by an orientation program given by another nurse and quickly found my place on the patient care team. I had never experienced such an orientation in England.   8.

Policy, drug reference, and procedure books at the nurses' station provide a ready reference where a nurse may check facts when she is in doubt, and she can instruct a new nurse on the staff without confusion. The active U.S. nurse, while working, can keep informed about new trends, discoveries, and inventions in a rapidly changing world of medicine.   9.

Here in the United States the nurse is regarded as an individual person and her personal life outside the hospital is given consideration. She develops interests in art, sport or a creative hobby; she is encouraged to further her education. Time and means are available to her to expand her horizons and to enrich her personality. Many nurses combine marriage and a career very ably in this country, but not in England or Ireland. All this tends to involve her more with people other than the sick. She is an interesting, informed, and happy person and at the bedside she can show understanding and perception.   10.

In Britain, like most nurses, I lived in a nurses' home on the hospital   11.

grounds and was thus isolated in a special hospital community. Theoretically I worked eight hours each day that I was on duty. But these hours were so arranged that one went to work twice in one day. One might work four hours in the morning, have a few hours free, and then go back to the ward for the evening. This schedule demands most of one's waking hours, and so mingling in the larger community outside the hospital was quite limited. The nurse was expected to find full satisfaction in her vocation, and thoughts of increases in salary were considered unworthy. Now, such attitudes are beginning to change and the winds of unrest are blowing through nursing in England, ruffling many a well-placed cap.

Discussion Questions: Essay 5

(Comparison or Contrast—*Madden*)

1. What kind of introduction does the author use?
2. Is this a comparison or contrast essay?
3. Which format, block or alternating, does Madden adhere to?
4. The number of paragraphs for each point varies throughout the essay. Also, the author does not follow a consistent A/B (Great Britain/United States, Great Britain/United States) pattern. Keeping this in mind, what are the areas that Madden focuses on in her discussion of nursing practices?
5. What technique does the author use to close the essay?

ESSAY 6: CLASSIFICATION ⎯⎯⎯⎯⎯⎯⎯⎯⎯⎯⎯

Salutation Displays

DESMOND MORRIS

1.   A Salutation Display demonstrates that we wish people well, or, at the very least, that we wish them no harm. It transmits signals of friendliness or the absence of hostility. It does this at peak moments—when people are arriving on the scene, departing from it, or dramatically changing their social role. We salute their comings, their goings and their transformations, and we do it with rituals of greeting, farewell and celebration.

2.   Whenever two friends meet after a long separation, they go through a special Greeting Ritual. During the first moments of the reunion they amplify their friendly signals to super-friendly signals. They smile and touch, often embrace and kiss, and generally behave more intimately and expansively than usual. They do this because they have to make up for lost time—lost friendship time. While they have been apart it has been impossible for them to send the hundreds of small, minute-by-minute friendly signals to each other that their relationship requires, and they have, so to speak, built up a backlog of these signals.

3.   This backlog amounts to a gestural debt that must be repaid without delay, as an assurance that the bond of friendship has not waned but has survived

the passage of time spent apart—hence the gushing ceremonies of the reunion scene, which must try to pay off this debt in a single outburst of activity.

Once the Greeting Ritual is over, the old relationship between the friends is now re-established and they can continue with their amicable interactions as before. Eventually, if they have to part for another long spell, there will be a Separation Ritual in which the super-friendly signals will once again be displayed. This time they have the function of leaving both partners with a powerful dose of befriendedness, to last them throughout the isolated times to come.

4.

In a similar way, if people undergo a major change in social role, we again offer them a massive outpouring of friendliness, because we are simultaneously saying farewell to their old self and greeting their new self. We do this when boy and girl become man and wife, when man and wife become father and mother, when prince becomes king, when candidate becomes president, and when competitor becomes champion.

5.

We have many formal procedures for celebrating these occasions, both the physical arrivals and departures and the symbolic comings and goings of the social transformations. We celebrate birthdays, christenings, comings-of age, weddings, coronations, anniversaries, inaugurations, presentations, and re-tirements. We give house-warmings, welcoming parties, farewell dinners, and funerals. In all these cases we are, in essence, performing Salutation Displays.

6.

The grander the occasion, the more rigid and institutional are the proce-dures. But even our more modest, private, two-person rituals follow distinct sets of rules. We seem to be almost incapable of beginning or ending any kind of encounter without performing some type of salutation. This is even true when we write a letter to someone. We begin with "Dear Mr. Smith" and end "Yours faithfully," and the rules of salutation are so compelling that we do this even when Mr. Smith is far from dear to us and we have little faith in him.

7.

Similarly we shake hands with unwelcome guests and express regret at their departure, although we are glad to see the back of them. All the more rea-son, then, that our genuine greetings and farewells should be excessively demonstrative.

8.

Social greetings that are planned and anticipated have a distinctive struc-ture and fall into four separate phases:

9.

1. The Inconvenience Display. To show the strength of our friendliness, we "put ourselves out" to varying degrees. We demonstrate that we are taking trouble. For both host and guest, this may mean "dressing up." For the guest it may mean a long journey. For the host it also entails a bodily shift from the center of his home territory. The stronger the greeting, the greater the inconven-ience. The Head of State drives to the airport to meet the important arrival. The brother drives to the airport to greet his sister returning from abroad. This is the maximum form of bodily displacement that a host can offer. From this extreme there is a declining scale of inconvenience, as the distance traveled by the host decreases. He may only go as far as the local station or bus depot. Or he may move no farther than his front drive, emerging from his front door after watching through the window for the moment of arrival. Or he may wait for the bell to ring and then only displace himself as far as his doorway or front hall. Or he may allow a child or servant to answer the door and remain in his room, the very center of his territory, awaiting the guest who is then ushered into his pres-

10.

ence. The minimal Inconvenience Display he can offer is to stand up when the guest enters the room, displacing himself vertically but not horizontally. Only if he remains seated as the guest enters and approaches him, can he be said to be totally omitting Phase One of a planned social greeting. Such omissions are extremely rare today and some degree of voluntary inconvenience is nearly always demonstrated. If, because of some accident or delay, it is unavoidably omitted, there are profuse apologies for its absence when the meeting finally takes place.

11.   At the time of farewell, the Inconvenience Display is repeated in much the same form. "You know your own way out" is the lowest level of expression here. Beyond that, there is an increasing displacement from territorial base, with the usual social level being "I will see you to the door." A slightly more intense form involves going outside the house and waiting there until the departing figures have vanished from sight. And so on, with the full expression being an accompaniment to the station or airport.

12.   2. The Distant Display. The main moment of greeting is when body contact is made, but before this comes the moment of first sighting. As soon as host and guest have identified each other, they signify this fact with a recognition response. Doorstep meetings tend to curtail this phase, because contact can be made almost immediately the door is opened, but in most other greeting situations the Distance Display is prominently demonstrated. It consists of six visual elements: (1) the Smile; (2) the Eyebrow Flash; (3) the Head Tilt; (4) the Hail; (5) the Wave; and (6) the Intention Embrace.

13.   The first three of these almost always occur, and they are performed simultaneously. At the moment of recognition, the head tilts back, the eyebrows arch up, and the face breaks into a large smile. The Head Tilt and the Eyebrow Flash may be very brief. They are elements of surprise. Combined with the smile, they signal a "pleasant surprise" at seeing the friend. This basic pattern may or may not be augmented by an arm movement. The simplest such action is the Hail—the raising of one hand. A more intense version, typical of long-distance greetings, is the Wave, and a still more intense expression is the Intention Embrace, in which the arms are stretched out towards the friend, as if the greeter cannot wait to perform the contact-embrace that is about to take place. A flamboyant specialty sometimes added is the Thrown or Blown Kiss, again anticipating the contact to come.

14.   As before, the same actions are repeated during the farewell Separation Ritual, but with Intention Embraces less likely and Thrown or Blown Kisses more likely.

15.   Of these Distant Displays, the Smile, Head Tilt, and Eyebrow Flash appear to be worldwide. They have been observed in remote native tribes that have never previously encountered white men. The raising of an arm in some form of Hail or Wave salute is also extremely widespread. The exact form of the arm movement may vary from culture to culture, but the existence of *some* kind of arm action appears to be global for mankind. The action seems to stem, like the Intention Embrace, from an urge to reach out and touch the other person. In the Hail, the arm is raised up rather than reached out, because this makes it more conspicuous from a distance, but the movement is essentially a stylized version of touching the distant friend. More "historical" explanations, such as that the

hand is raised to show it empty of weapons or that it is thrust up to mime the action of offering the owner's sword, and therefore his allegiance, may be true in certain specific contexts, but the action is too widespread and too general for this interpretation to stand for all cases of Hailing.

The Wave takes three main forms: the Vertical Wave, the Hidden-palm Wave, and the Lateral Wave. In the Vertical Wave, the palm faces the friend and the hand moves repeatedly up and down. This appears to be the "primitive" form of waving. In origin, it seems to be a vacuum patting action, the hand patting the friend's body at a distance, again in anticipation of the friendly embrace to come. The Hidden-palm Wave, seen mainly in Italy, is also a patting action, but with the hand moving repeatedly towards the waver himself. To non-Italians, this looks rather like beckoning, but it is basically another form of vacuum embracing. The Lateral Wave, common all over the world consists of showing the palm to the friend and then moving it rhythmically from side to side. This appears to be an improved form of the other waves. The modification is essentially one of increasing the visibility and conspicuousness of the patting action. In turning it into a lateral movement, it loses its embracing quality, but gains dramatically in visual impact from a distance. It can be further exaggerated by extending it to full arm-waving, or even double-arm-waving.

3. The Close Display. As soon as the Distant Display has been performed, there is an approach interval and then the key moment of actual body contact. At full intensity this consists of a total embrace, bringing both arms around the friend's body, with frontal trunk contact and head contact. There is much hugging, squeezing, patting, cheek-pressing, and kissing. This may be followed by intense eye contact at close range, cheek-clasping, mouth-kissing, hair-stroking, laughing, even weeping, and, of course, continued smiling.

From this uninhibited display, there is a whole range of body-contacts of decreasing strength, right down to the formal handshake. The precise intensity will depend on: (1) the depth of the prior relationship; (2) the length of the separation; (3) the privacy of the greeting context; (4) the local, cultural display-rules and traditions; and (5) the changes that have taken place during the separation.

Most of these conditions are obvious enough, but the last deserves comment. If the friend is known to have been through some major emotional experience—an ordeal such as imprisonment, illness, or disaster, or a great success such as an award, a victory, or an honor—there will be a much more intense greeting and stronger embracing. This is because the Salutation Display is simultaneously a greeting and a celebration and is, in effect, double-strength.

Different cultures have formalized the close greeting performance in different ways. In all cases, the basis of the display is the full embrace, but when this is simplified, different parts of it are retained in different places. In some cultures, the head-to-head element becomes nose-rubbing, cheek-mouthing, or face-pressing. In others, there is a stylized mutual cheek-kiss, with the lips stopping short of contact. In others again, there is kissing between men—in France and Russia, for example—while in many cultures, male-to-male kissing is omitted as supposedly effeminate.

While these cultural variations are, of course, of interest, they should not be allowed to obscure the fact that they are all variations on a basic theme—the body embrace. This is the fundamental, global, human contact action, the one

16.

17.

18.

19.

20.

21.

we all know as babies, infants, and growing children, and to which we return whenever the rules permit and we wish to demonstrate feelings of attachment for another individual.

22.   4. The "Grooming" Display. Following the initial body contacts, we move into the final stage of the greeting ceremony, which is similar to the social grooming performances of monkeys and apes. We do not pick at one another's fur, but instead we display "Grooming Talk"—inane comments that mean very little in themselves, but which demonstrate vocally our pleasure at the meeting. "How are you?" "How nice of you to come," "Did you have a good journey?" "You are looking so well," "Let me take your coat," and so on. The answers are barely heard. All that is important is to pay compliments and to receive them. To show concern and to show pleasure. The precise verbal content and the intelligence of the questions is almost irrelevant. This Grooming Display is sometimes augmented by helping with clothing, taking off coats, and generally fussing with creature comforts. On occasion there is an additional Gift Display on the part of the guest, who brings some small offering as a further, material form of salutation.

23.   After the Grooming Display is over, the friends leave the special site of the greeting and move on to resume their old, familiar, social interactions. The Salutation Display is complete and has performed its important task.

24.   By contrast, unplanned greetings are far less elaborate. When we see a friend in the street, or somewhere away from home, we give the typical Distant Display—a smile and a wave—and perhaps no more. Or we approach and add a Close Display, usually a rather abbreviated embrace, but more usually a mere handshake. As we part, we again display, often turning for a final Distant Signal, as we move off.

25.   Introductory Greetings take yet another form. If we are meeting someone for the first time, we omit the Distant Display, simply because we are not recognizing an old friend. We do, however, offer a minor form of Close Display, nearly always a handshake, and we smile at the new acquaintance and offer him a Grooming Display of friendly chatter and concern. We treat him, in fact, as though he were a friend already, not a close one but a friend none the less, and in so doing we bring him into our orbit and initiate a social relationship with him.

26.   As a species of primate, we are remarkably rich in greetings and farewells. Other primates do show some simple greeting rituals, but we exceed them all, and we also show farewell displays which they seem to lack entirely. Looking back into our ancestry, there seems to have been a good reason for this development. Most primates move around in a fairly close-knit group. Occasionally, they may drift apart and then, on reuniting, will give small gestures of greeting. But they rarely part deliberately, in a purposeful way, so they have no use for Separation Displays. Early man established himself as a hunting species, with the male hunting group leaving for a specific purpose at a specific time, and then returning to the home base with the kill. For millions of years, therefore, we have needed Salutation Displays, both in the form of farewells, as the group split up in its major division-of-labor, and in the form of greetings, when they came together again. And the importance of success or failure on the hunt meant that these were not trivial, but vital moments in the communal life of the primeval tribe. Little wonder that today we are such a salutatory species.

Discussion Questions: Essay 6

(Classification—*Morris*)

1. Paragraph 1 introduces the general topic of this essay. Where is the thesis actually found?
2. What is the purpose of paragraphs 2 through 8? Why are these paragraphs necessary?
3. In the body of this essay, Morris does not use transitions between paragraphs. He uses numbers and titles for each display. What are some reasons he did this instead of using topic sentences?
4. Why does the Inconvenience Display have two paragraphs?
5. The Distant Display is divided into six elements. One of these elements, the Wave, is further divided into three main forms. How does Morris manage to keep these subdivisions clear?
6. Are paragraphs 24 and 25 really needed? Why do you think the author chose to include them?
7. The closing paragraph finishes this essay nicely. Why does it strengthen the essay?

ESSAY 7: CAUSE OR EFFECT

The Electronic Revolution
ARTHUR C. CLARKE

The electron is the smallest thing in the universe; it would take thirty thousand million, million, million, million of them to make a single ounce. Yet this utterly invisible, all but weightless object has given us powers over nature of which our ancestors never dreamed. The electron is our most ubiquitous slave; without its aid, our civilization would collapse in a moment, and humanity would revert to scattered bands of starving, isolated savages.

1.

We started to use the electron fifty years before we discovered it. The first practical application of electricity (which is nothing more than the ordered movement of electrons) began with the introduction of the telegraph in the 1840's. With really astonishing speed, a copper cobweb of wires and cables spread across the face of the world, and the abolition of distance had begun. For over a century we have taken the instantaneous transfer of news completely for granted; it is very hard to believe that when Lincoln was born, communications were little faster than in the days of Julius Caesar.

2.

Although the beginning of "electronics" is usually dated around the 1920's, this represents a myopic view of technology. With the hindsight of historical perspective, we can now see that the telegraph and the telephone are the first two landmarks of the electronic age. After Alexander Graham Bell had sent his voice from one room to another in 1876, society could never be the same again. For the telephone was the first electronic device to enter the home and to affect directly the lives of ordinary men and women, giving them the almost

3.

godlike power of projecting their personalities and thoughts from point to point with the speed of lightning.

4.   Until the closing years of the nineteenth century, men used and handled electricity without knowing what it was, but in the 1890's they began to investigate its fundamental nature, by observing what happened when an electric current was passed through gases at very low pressures. One of the first, and most dramatic, results of this work was the invention of the X-ray tube, which may be regarded as the ancestor of all the millions of vacuum tubes which followed it. A cynic might also argue that it is the only electronic device wholly beneficial to mankind—though when it was invented many terrified spinsters, misunderstanding its powers, denounced poor Röntgen as a violator of privacy.

5.   There is an important lesson to be learned from the X-ray tube. If a scientist of the late Victorian era had been asked "In what way could money best be spent to further the progress of medicine?" he would never by any stretch of the imagination have replied: "By encouraging research on the conduction of electricity through rarefied gases." Yet that is what would have been the right answer, for until the discovery of X rays doctors and surgeons were like blind men, groping in the dark. One can never predict the outcome of fundamental scientific research, or guess what remote and unexpected fields of knowledge it will illuminate.

6.   X rays were discovered in 1895—the electron itself just one year later. It was then realized that an electric current consists of myriads of these submicroscopic particles, each carrying a minute negative charge. When a current flows through a solid conductor such as a piece of copper wire, we may imagine the electrons creeping like grains of sand through the interstices between the (relatively) boulder-sized copper atoms. Any individual electron does not move very far, or very fast, but it jostles its neighbor and so the impulse travels down the line at speeds of thousands of miles a second. Thus when we switch on a light, or send a Morse dash across the transatlantic cable, the response at the other end is virtually instantaneous.

7.   But electrons can also travel *without* wires to guide them, when they shoot across the empty space of a vacuum tube like a hail of machine-gun bullets. Under these conditions, no longer entangled in solid matter, they are very sensitive to the pull and tug of electric fields, and as a result can be used to amplify faint signals. You demonstrate the principle involved every time you hold a hose-pipe in your hand; the slightest movement of your wrist produces a much greater effect at the far end of the jet. Something rather similar happens to the beam of electrons crossing the space in a vacuum tube; they can thus multiply a millionfold the feeble impulses picked up by a radio antenna, or paint a fluorescent picture on the end of a television screen.

8.   Until 1948, electronics was almost synonymous with the vacuum tube. The entire development of radio, talkies, radar, television, long-distance telephony, up to that date depended upon little glass bottles containing intricate structures of wire and mica. By the late 1940's the vacuum tube had shrunk from an object as large as (and sometimes almost as luminous as) an electric light bulb, to a cylinder not much bigger than a man's thumb. Then three scientists at the Bell Telephone Laboratories invented the transistor and we moved from the Paleoelectronic to the Neoelectronic Age.

Though the transistor is so small—its heart is a piece of crystal about the size of a rice grain—it does everything that a radio tube can do. However, it requires only a fraction of the power and space, and is potentially much more reliable. Indeed, it is hard to see how a properly designed transistor can ever wear out; think of little Vanguard I, still beeping away up there in space, and liable to continue indefinitely until some exasperated astronaut scoops it up with a butterfly net.

9.

The transistor is of such overwhelming importance because it (and its still smaller successors) makes practical hundreds of electronic devices which were previously too bulky, too expensive or too unreliable for everyday use. The pocket radio is a notorious example; whether we like it or not, it points the way inevitably to a day when person-to-person communications is universal. Then everyone in the world will have his individual telephone number, perhaps given to him at birth and serving all the other needs of an increasingly complex society (driving license, social security, credit card, permit to have additional children, etc.). You may not know where on Earth your friend Joe Smith may be at any particular moment; but you will be able to dial him instantly—if only you can remember whether his number is 8296765043 or 8296756043.

10.

Obviously, there are both advantages and disadvantages in such a "personalized" communication system; the solitude which we all need at some time in our lives will join the vanished silences of the pre-jet age. Against this, there is no other way in which a really well-informed *and* fast-reacting democratic society can be achieved on the original Greek plan—with direct participation of every citizen in the affairs of the state. The organization of such a society, with feedback in both directions from the humblest citizen to the President of the World, is a fascinating exercise in political planning. As usual, it is an exercise that will not be completed by the time we need the answers.

11.

A really efficient and universal communications system, giving high-quality reception on all bands between all points on the Earth, can be achieved only with the aid of satellites. As they come into general use, providing enormous information-handling capacity on a global basis, today's patterns of business, education, entertainment, international affairs will change out of all recognition. Men will be able to meet face to face (individually, or in groups) without ever leavng their homes, by means of closed circuit television. As a result of this, the enormous amount of commuting and traveling that now takes place from home to office, from ministry to United Nations, from university to conference hall will steadily decrease. There are administrators, scientists and businessmen today who spend about a third of their working lives either traveling or preparing to travel. Much of this is stimulating, but most of it is unnecessary and exhausting.

12.

The improvement of communications will also render obsolete the city's historic role as a meeting place for minds and a center of social intercourse. This is just as well anyway, since within another generation most of our cities will be strangled to death by their own traffic.

13.

But though electronics will ultimately separate men from their jobs, so that (thanks to remote manipulation devices) not even a brain surgeon need be within five thousand miles of his patient, it must also be recognized that few of today's jobs will survive long into the electronic age. It is now a cliché that we are

14.

entering the Second Industrial Revolution, which involves the mechanization not of energy, but of thought. Like all clichés this is so true that we seldom stop to analylze what it means.

15.   It means nothing less than this: There are no routine, noncreative activities of the human mind which cannot be carried out by suitably designed machines. The development of computers to supervise industrial processes, commercial transactions and even military operations has demonstrated this beyond doubt. Yet today's computers are morons compared to those that they themselves are now helping to design.

16.   I would not care to predict how many of today's professions will survive a hundred years from now. What happened to the buggywhip makers, the crossing sweepers, the scriveners, the stonebreakers of yesteryear? (I mention the last because I can just remember them, hammering away at piles of rock in the country lanes of my childhood.) Most of our present occupations will follow these into oblivion, as the transistor inherits the earth.

17.   For as computers become smaller, cheaper and more reliable they will move into every field of human activity. Today they are in the office; tomorrow they will be in the home. Indeed, some very simpleminded computers already do our household chores; the device that programs a washing machine to perform a certain sequence of operations is a specialized mechanical brain. Less specialized ones would be able to carry out almost all the routine operations in a suitably designed house.

18.   Because we have so many more pressing problems on our hands, only the science-fiction writers—those trail-blazers of the future—have given much thought to the social life of the later electronic age. How will our descendants be educated for leisure, when the working week is only a few hours? We have already seen, on a worldwide scale, the cancerous growths resulting from idleness and lack of usable skills. At every street corner in a great city you will find lounging groups of leather-jacketed, general-purpose bioelectric computers of a performance it will take us centuries and trillions of dollars to match. What is their future—and ours?

19.   More than half a century ago H. G. Wells described, in *The Time Machine,* a world of decadent pleasure lovers, bereft of goals and ambitions, sustained by subterranean machines. He set his fantasy eight hundred thousand years in the future, but we may reach a similar state of affairs within a dozen generations. No one who contemplates the rising curve of technology from the Pilgrim fathers to the Apollo Project dare deny that this is not merely possible, but probable.

20.   For most of history, men have been producers; in a very few centuries, they will have to switch to the role of consumers devoting their energies 100 per cent to absorbing the astronomical output of the automated mines, farms and factories.

21.   Does this *really* matter, since only a tiny fraction of the human race has ever contributed to artistic creation, scientific discovery or philosophical thought, which in the long run are the only significant activities of mankind? Archimedes and Aristotle, one cannot help thinking, would still have left their marks on history even if they had lived in a society based on robots instead of human slaves. In any culture, they would be consumers of goods, but producers of thought.

We should not take too much comfort from this. The electronic computers of today are like the subhuman primates of ten million years ago, who could have given any visiting Martians only the faintest hints of their potentialities, which included the above mentioned Archimedes and Aristotle. Evolution is swifter now; electronic intelligence is only decades, not millions of years, ahead.

22.

And *that*—not transistor radios, automatic homes, global TV—is the ultimate goal of the Electronic Revolution. Whether we like it or not, we are on a road where there is no turning back; and waiting at its end are our successors.

23.

Discussion Questions: Essay 7

(Cause or Effect—*Clarke*)

1. Is this a cause or effect essay?
2. Why does the first paragraph open this essay effectively?
3. You might think that the thesis statement is the last sentence in paragraph 1, yet it is not a direct statement. What is the implied thesis? Although you probably do not want to do this in your own essays, why do you think Clarke did not include a direct thesis?
4. Paragraphs 2 through 10 give a chronological presentation of the development of electronics. Although these paragraphs may not seem necessary in this essay, they lend support to the main idea of the final few paragraphs. How are these two sections related?
5. The body paragraphs begin with paragraph 11. Clarke presents at least five main points. What are they?
6. Although many effects of the electronic revolution are actually happening today, they are presented as occurring in the future. Again, although you will probably not want to do this in your own essays, Clarke did this for a purpose. It is to prepare the reader for what Clarke perceives as the most important effect. This effect is found in the two closing paragraphs. What is it?
7. Although the final effect is a sixth effect, it also operates effectively as a closing. What method of closing is Clarke using?

ESSAY 8: PROCESS

An Amish Wedding

JOHN HOSTETLER

A wedding in Amish life is an elaborate affair, for the whole community has a stake in marriage. For the community it means a new home, another place to have preaching when the couple is located on the farm, and another family to raise children in the Amish way. Marriage also means that the young couple is ready to part with their juvenile and sometimes wild behavior and to settle down to keeping the faith in a mature way. For the couple itself marriage

1.

is a rite of passage marking the passing from youth into the age of adult responsibility.

2.   Amish courtship is secretive, and the community at large is not to know about an intended wedding until the couple is "published" in church, usually two Sundays before the wedding. Signs of an approaching wedding, however, provide occasion for joking and teasing. Since there is nothing among the Amish that corresponds to the engagement, other signs of preparation become indicative of a potential marriage. An overabundance of celery in the garden of a home containing a potential bride is said to be one such sign, since large quantities are used at weddings. Another cue may be efforts on the part of the father of the potential bridegroom to obtain an extra farm, or to remodel a vacant dwelling on one of his own farms.

3.   Weddings are traditionally held in November and December, since this is a time when the work year allows community-wide participation. The great amount of preparation requires that weddings be held during the week, usually on a Thursday, or on Tuesday if there are conflicting dates with other marriages. Second marriages or those involving older persons may be held anytime during the year and often do not involve such elaborate preparations.

4.   Shortly before a young man wishes to be married he approaches the deacon or a minister of his choosing and makes known his desires. The official then becomes the *Schteckleimann* or go-between. His task is to go secretly, usually after dark, to the home of the bridegroom's fiancée and verify her wishes for marriage and to obtain the consent of her parents. Of course the girl and her parents have by this time already given informal consent, so that the duty of the intermediary is little more than a formality.

5.   The deacon reports his findings to the bishop who announces or "publishes" the intent of the couple at the next preaching service. The bridegroom-to-be, who is always present at this service, leaves immediately after the important announcement, just before the last hymn is sung. He hitches his horse and is off to the home of his fiancée, where she is awaiting the news that they have been "published."

6.   After being "published" the bridegroom lives at the bride's home until the wedding day. They are busy during this time with the innumerable preparations that must be made. Walnuts and hickory nuts need to be cracked, floors scrubbed, furniture moved, silverware polished, and dishes borrowed.

7.   The bridegroom's first assignment is to invite personally all of the wedding guests. He sets out in his buggy early Monday morning to invite two hundred or more friends, relatives, and neighbors agreed upon informally by the parents of the couple. No wedding invitations are mailed. Invitations include entire families, or certain members of the family, such as the husband or wife only. Children are specifically mentioned if they are invited. Some are invited only for the evening. Honorary invitations are extended to uncles, aunts, and neighbors to serve as cooks. Both men and their wives serve in this capacity. The parents of the bridal party decide who shall be invited to the wedding and who shall have special honors in serving the meal.

8.   Wedding customs vary from one ceremonial and ecological community to another, especially in menu, physical arrangements, and whether games are played. The following are observations made by the writer at a wedding in central Pennsylvania.

Large-scale preparations began on the day before the wedding. The cooks, married couples numbering thirty persons in all, began to arrive at the bride's home at seven o'clock in the morning. Custom requires that the bridegroom cut off the heads of the fowl. Men picked the chickens, ducks, and turkeys. The women washed and dressed them. The women prepared the dressing, stuffed the fowl, washed dishes, baked quantities of pies, peeled two bushels of potatoes, and cracked nuts. The men cleaned celery, supplied plenty of hot water from large kettles, emptied garbage, and constructed temporary tables for the main rooms in the house. These tables, made of wide pine boards and trestles, were placed around three sides of the living room. Two tables were in the kitchen and one in the bedroom, making the equivalent of about six tables with a total seating capacity of one hundred. The dressed, stuffed fowl were placed in the large outside bake oven on the evening before the wedding.

9.

The wedding day itself was a great occasion not only for the bride and bridegroom, but for the kinship community and guests, especially the young people. Before daylight on the day of the wedding the bride and bridegroom and their two attending couples went to a neighbor's place a mile from the bride's home where the preaching and ceremony were to take place. A usual four-hour preaching service was held for the event, lasting from nine in the morning to one o'clock in the afternoon. This service was open to the public, but was attended chiefly by those who were invited to the wedding.

10.

As wedding guests arrived for the service the bridal party was already sitting in the front row. When the house was filled, the ministers proceeded to the council room and the bride and groom followed. Here they were given private instructions concerning the duties of marriage, while the assembly below sang wedding hymns (*Ausbund*, selections 97, 69, 131). Upon returning to the assembly the bridal party (holding hands) took their special seats near the ministers' row, the three young men facing their partners. Their clothes were new, but typical of their regular Sunday garb. The main sermon delivered by the bishop focused on marriages in the Old Testament: the story of Adam and Eve, the wickedness of mankind after the flood in that "they took them wives of all which they chose," the uprightness of Noah's household in not intermarrying with unbelievers, the story of Isaac and Rebecca, and the adulterous plight of Solomon. The sermon was concluded with a rehearsal of the story of Tobias (from the Apocrypha) and how he got his wife. Two passages of Scripture were read with little comment.

11.

Near the hour of twelve noon and at the end of his long sermon, the bishop asked the couple to come forward if it was still their desire to be united in matrimony. The ceremony was completed without the aid of a book or written notes. It consisted of a few questions and responses and concluded with the bishop placing his hands on the clasped hands of the couple as he pronounced a blessing upon them.

12.

Discussion Questions: Essay 8

(Process—*Hostetler*)

1. The first sentence of the essay might be seen as the thesis statement, but it really is not. Although it talks about the importance

of weddings in the Amish life, this is not the thesis. Write an appropriate thesis statement for the essay.

2. Is this an explanatory or informational process?

3. There are four main phases in this essay: secret actions, host-
"published" actions, the day-before preparations, and the
wedding-day activities. Identify the major steps in each of these
phases.

4. Paragraphs 3 and 8 are not really steps in the process. Why, then,
did the author think them important enough to include in the essay? What purpose do they serve?

5. One of the impressive aspects of this essay is the abundance of
detail. Paragraphs 7 and 9 are good examples of the use of detail.
Why do these details help the essay so much?

6. This essay does not have a formal closing paragraph. How does
the author create a sense of conclusion?

ESSAY 9: EXTENDED DEFINITION

The Concept of Culture

CLYDE KLUCKHOHN

1.   Why do the Chinese dislike milk and milk products? Why would the Japanese die willingly in a Banzai charge that seemed senseless to Americans? Why
do some nations trace descent through the father, others through the mother,
still others through both parents? Not because different peoples have different
instincts, not because they were destined by God or Fate to different habits, not
because the weather is different in China and Japan and the United States.
Sometimes shrewd common sense has an answer that is close to that of the
anthropologist: "because they were brought up that way." By "culture" anthropology means the total life way of a people, the social legacy the individual ac-
quires from his group. Or culture can be regarded as that part of the environment that is the creation of man.

2.   This technical term has a wider meaning than the "culture" of history and
literature. A humble cooking pot is as much a cultural product as is a Beethoven
sonata. In ordinary speech a man of culture is a man who can speak languages
other than his own, who is familiar with history, literature, philosophy, or the fine
arts. In some cliques that definition is still narrower. The cultured person is one
who can talk about James Joyce, Scarlatti, and Picasso. To the anthropologist,
however, to be human is to be cultured. There is a culture in general, and then
there are the specific cultures such as Russian, American, British, Hottentot,
Inca. The general abstract notion serves to remind us that we cannot explain
acts solely in terms of the biological properties of the people concerned, their
individual past experience, and the immediate situation. The past experience of
other men in the form of culture enters into almost every event. Each specific
culture constitutes a kind of blueprint for all of life's activities.

3.   One of the interesting things about human beings is that they try to under-

stand themselves and their own behavior. While this has been particularly true of Europeans in recent times, there is no group which has not developed a scheme or schemes to explain man's actions. To the insistent human query "why?" the most exciting illumination anthropology has to offer is that of the concept of culture. Its explanatory importance is comparable to categories such as evolution in biology, gravity in physics, disease in medicine. A good deal of human behavior can be understood, and indeed predicted, if we know a people's design for living. Many acts are neither accidental nor due to personal peculiarities nor caused by supernatural forces nor simply mysterious. Even those of us who pride ourselves on our individualism follow most of the time a pattern not of our own making. We brush our teeth on arising. We put on pants—not a loincloth or a grass skirt. We eat three meals a day—not four or five or two. We sleep in a bed—not a hammock or on a sheep pelt. I do not have to know the individual and his life history to be able to predict these and countless other regularities, including many in the thinking process, of all Americans who are not incarcerated in jails or hospitals for the insane.

4. To the American woman a system of plural wives seems "instinctively" abhorrent. She cannot understand how any woman can fail to be jealous and uncomfortable if she must share her husband with other women. She feels it "unnatural" to accept such a situation. On the other hand, a Koryak woman of Siberia, for example, would find it hard to understand how a woman could be so selfish and so undesirous of feminine companionship in the home as to wish to restrict her husband to one mate.

5. Some years ago I met in New York City a young man who did not speak a word of English and was obviously bewildered by American ways. By "blood" he was as American as you or I, for his parents had gone from Indiana to China as missionaries. Orphaned in infancy, he was reared by a Chinese family in a remote village. All who met him found him more Chinese than American. The facts of his blue eyes and light hair were less impressive than a Chinese style of gait, Chinese arm and hand movements, Chinese facial expression, and Chinese modes of thought. The biological heritage was American, but the cultural training had been Chinese. He returned to China. Another example of another kind: I once knew a trader's wife in Arizona who took a somewhat devilish interest in producing a cultural reaction. Guests who came her way were often served delicious sandwiches filled with a meat that seemed to be neither chicken nor tuna fish yet was reminiscent of both. To queries she gave no reply until each had eaten his fill. She then explained that what they had eaten was not chicken, not tuna fish, but the rich, white flesh of freshly killed rattlesnakes. The response was instantaneous—vomiting, often violent vomiting. A biological process is caught in a cultural web.

6. A highly intelligent teacher with long and successful experience in the public schools of Chicago was finishing her first year in an Indian school. When asked how her Navaho pupils compared in intelligence with Chicago youngsters, she replied, "Well I just don't know. Sometimes the Indians seem just as bright. At other times they just act like dumb animals. The other night we had a dance in the high school. I saw a boy who is one of the best students in my English class standing off by himself. So I took him over to a pretty girl and told them to dance. But they just stood there with their heads down. They wouldn't

even say anything." I inquired if she knew whether or not they were members of the same clan. "What difference would that make?"

7.   "How would you feel about getting into bed with your brother?" The teacher walked off in a huff, but, actually, the two cases were quite comparable in principle. To the Indian the type of bodily contact involved in our social dancing has a directly sexual connotation. The incest taboos between members of the same clan are as severe as between true brothers and sisters. The shame of the Indians at the suggestion that a clan brother and sister should dance and the indignation of the white teacher at the idea that she should share a bed with an adult brother represent equally nonrational responses, culturally standardized unreason.

8.   All this does not mean that there is no such thing as raw human nature. The very fact that certain of the same institutions are found in all known societies indicates that at bottom all human beings are very much alike. The files of the Cross-Cultural Survey at Yale University are organized according to categories such as "marriage ceremonies," "life crisis rites," "incest taboos." At least seventy-five of these categories are represented in every single one of the hundreds of cultures analyzed. This is hardly surprising. The members of all human groups have about the same biological equipment. All men undergo the same poignant life experiences such as birth, helplessness, illness, old age, and death. The biological potentialities of the species are the blocks with which cultures are built. Some patterns of every culture crystallize around focuses provided by the inevitables of biology: the difference between the sexes, the presence of persons of different ages, the varying physical strength and skill of individuals. The facts of nature also limit culture forms. No culture provides patterns for jumping over trees or for eating iron ore.

9.   There is thus no "either-or" between nature and that special form of nurture called culture. Culture determinism is as one-sided as biological determinism. The two factors are interdependent. Culture arises out of human nature, and its forms are restricted both by man's biology and by natural laws. It is equally true that culture channels biological processes—vomiting, weeping, fainting, sneezing, the daily habits of food intake and waste elimination. When a man eats, he is reacting to an internal "drive," namely, hunger contractions consequent upon the lowering of blood sugar, but his precise reaction to these internal stimuli cannot be predicted by physiological knowledge alone. Whether a healthy adult feels hungry twice, three times, or four times a day and the hours at which this feeling recurs is a question of culture. *What* he eats is of course limited by availability, but is also partly regulated by culture. It is a biological fact that some types of berries are poisonous; it is a cultural fact that, a few generations ago, most Americans considered tomatoes to be poisonous and refused to eat them. Such selective, discriminative use of the environment is characteristically cultural. In a still more general sense, too, the process of eating is channeled by culture. Whether a man eats to live, lives to eat, or merely eats and lives is only in part an individual matter, for there are also cultural trends. Emotions are physiological events. Certain situations will evoke fear in people from any culture. But sensations of pleasure, anger, and lust may be stimulated by cul-

tural cues that would leave unmoved someone who has been reared in a different social tradition.

Except in the case of newborn babies and of individuals born with clear-cut structural or functional abnormalities we can observe innate endowments only as modified by cultural training. In a hospital in New Mexico where Zuñi Indian, Navaho Indian, and white American babies are born, it is possible to classify the newly arrived infants as unusually active, average, and quiet. Some babies from each "racial" group will fall into each category, though a higher proportion of the white babies will fall into the unusually active class. But if a Navaho baby, a Zuñi baby, and a white baby—all classified as unusually active at birth—are again observed at the age of two years, the Zuñi baby will no longer seem given to quick and restless activity—*as compared with the white child*—though he may seem so as compared with the other Zuñis of the same age. The Navaho child is likely to fall in between as contrasted with the Zuñi and the white, though he will probably still seem more active than the average Navaho youngster.   10.

It was remarked by many observers in the Japanese relocation centers that Japanese who were born and brought up in this country, especially those who were reared apart from any large colony of Japanese, resemble in behavior their white neighbors much more closely than they do their own parents who were educated in Japan.   11.

I have said "culture channels biological processes." It is more accurate to say "the biological functioning of individuals is modified if they have been trained in certain ways and not in others." Culture is not a disembodied force. It is created and transmitted by people. However, culture, like well-known concepts of the physical sciences, is a convenient abstraction. One never sees gravity. One sees bodies falling in regular ways. One never sees an electromagnetic field. Yet certain happenings that can be seen may be given a neat abstract formulation by assuming that the electromagnetic field exists. Similarly, one never sees culture as such. What is seen are regularities in the behavior or artifacts of a group that has adhered to a common tradition. The regularities in style and technique of ancient Inca tapestries or stone axes from Melanesian islands are due to the existence of mental blueprints for the group.   12.

Culture is a way of thinking, feeling, believing. It is the group's knowledge stored up (in memories of men; in books and objects) for future use. We study the products of this "mental" activity: the overt behavior, the speech and gestures and activities of people, and the tangible results of these things such as tools, houses, cornfields, and what not. It has been customary in lists of "culture traits" to include such things as watches or lawbooks. This is a convenient way of thinking about them, but in the solution of any important problem we must remember that they, in themselves, are nothing but metals, paper, and ink. What is important is that some men know how to make them, others set a value on them, are unhappy without them, direct their activities in relation to them, or disregard them.   13.

. . .

Since culture is an abstraction, it is important not to confuse culture with   14.

society. A "society" refers to a group of people who interact more with each other than they do with other individuals—who cooperate with each other for the attainment of certain ends. You can see and indeed count the individuals who make up a society. A "culture" refers to the distinctive ways of life of such a group of people. Not all social events are culturally patterned. New types of circumstances arise for which no cultural solutions have as yet been devised.

15.   A culture constitutes a storehouse of the pooled learning of the group. A rabbit starts life with some innate responses. He can learn from his own experience and perhaps from observing other rabbits. A human infant is born with fewer instincts and greater plasticity. His main task is to learn the answers that persons he will never see, persons long dead, have worked out. Once he has learned the formulas supplied by the culture of his group, most of his behavior becomes almost as automatic and unthinking as if it were instinctive. There is a tremendous amount of intelligence behind the making of a radio, but not much is required to learn to turn it on.

      . . .

16.   A culture is learned by individuals as the result of belonging to some particular group, and it constitutes that part of learned behavior which is shared with others. It is our social legacy, as contrasted with our organic heredity. It is one of the important factors which permits us to live together in an organized society, giving us ready-made solutions to our problems, helping us to predict the behavior of others, and permitting others to know what to expect of us.

17.   Culture regulates our lives at every turn. From the moment we are born until we die there is, whether we are conscious of it or not, constant pressure upon us to follow certain types of behavior that other men have created for us. Some paths we follow willingly, others we follow because we know no other way, still others we deviate from or go back to most unwilingly. Mothers of small children know how unnaturally most of this comes to us—how little regard we have, until we are "culturalized," for the "proper" place, time, and manner for certain acts such as eating, excreting, sleeping, getting dirty, and making loud noises. But by more or less adhering to a system of related designs for carrying out all the acts of living, a group of men and women feel themselves linked together by a powerful chain of sentiments. Ruth Benedict gave an almost complete definition of the concept when she said, "Culture is that which binds men together."

Discussion Questions: Essay 9

(Extended Definition—*Kluckhohn*)

1. How does the author of this essay attract the reader's attention in his opening paragraph?
2. Since this is an extended definition, the thesis is a presentation of the term and its basic definition. Kluckhohn's definition, presented at the end of the first paragraph, is the anthropological one. What type of definition of culture does he give in paragraph 2?

3. Paragraphs 4 through 7 include several examples of how strongly culture is ingrained in individuals. Why does the author use so many examples?
4. How does the author use comparison and analogy to explain culture in paragraph 12?
5. In paragraph 14, how does the author help the reader understand what culture is?
6. What point is the author making in the two closing paragraphs? In other words, what type of closing does he use?

Index